The Monmouth County Park System

• T H E   F I R S T   F I F T Y   Y E A R S •

The Monmouth County Park System

· THE FIRST FIFTY YEARS ·

Clifford W. Zink

THE FRIENDS OF THE MONMOUTH COUNTY PARK SYSTEM · MONMOUTH COUNTY · NEW JERSEY

ISBN 978-0-615-35501-6

First Edition

Published and funded by The Friends of the Monmouth County Park System, Inc., a membership-based 501(c) (3) charitable organization that provides financial support exclusively for Monmouth County Park System enhancements, including historical and natural resource preservation, recreation for urban youth, and activities for individuals with disabilities within our community.

The Friends of the Monmouth County Park System
P.O. Box 686, Lincroft, N.J. 07738
Tel: (732) 975-9735

www.friendsofmonmouthcountyparks.com

Gregory Hunt, *President*
Maria Wojciechowski, *Executive Director*

Project Director: Gail L. Hunton
Book Design: Frank Mahood
Proofreader: Carol Maglio

Printed in the United States of America
Walsworth Print Group
306 North Kansas Avenue
Marceline, Missouri 64658

www.walsworthprinting.com

Dedication

THIS HISTORY of the Monmouth County Park System is dedicated to the men and women who have given their time and talents to create a nationally recognized open space, parks and recreation agency to serve their fellow citizens. Credit for the growth and success of the Park System belongs to many individuals over the past 50 years – farsighted County leaders, dedicated employees, generous donors, and supportive volunteers and non-profit organizations that enhance the services that we provide to the public. Every successful land preservation story and every beautiful park or recreation activity presented on these pages is the result of the actions of people who worked for the common good, and this book is a tribute to them.

This publication, written to commemorate the Park System's 50th anniversary, was made possible by The Friends of the Parks and the efforts of Park System staff. Special thanks go to Gail Hunton, Supervising Historic Preservation Specialist, who coordinated the development and editing of this publication, employees who provided information and photographs, Clifford W. Zink who researched and wrote the text, Frank Mahood who designed the book, and Carol Maglio who proof read the copy.

James J. Truncer, *Secretary-Director,*
Monmouth County Park System

Contents

Illustrations

WE SET OUT to illustrate the Monmouth County parks in this book with photographs taken by Park System employees, and the results have exceeded our expectations. Employees took the vast majority of the 423 photographs in this book, and the quality of their images shows both the excellent skills of these amateur photographers and their deep connections to the open spaces, facilities, and natural resources within the Park System.

Many of these employees anonymously provided their photographs to the Park System archives over the years. Many others have generously shared their photographs for this publication, and we especially thank Andrew Coeyman, Kelly Cole, Maribeth Gardner, Bruce Gollnick, Robert Henschel, Linda Hubbell, George Lentz, Mark Miller, Andi Monick, and Ken Thoman for their fine contributions. Robert Henschel, a long-time Park System naturalist, has photographed the parks for over 30 years and deserves special recognition for several of the signature images in this book. Clifford Zink also provided key photographs of several parks.

The task of assembling historical images for this book was especially challenging because the Thompson Park Visitor Center fire in 2006 destroyed hundreds of the Park System's photographs of parks, programs and people over many years. We thank all the Park System employees who hunted through their files to locate and reproduce images, and especially Cheryl-Stoeber Goff and Lisa Bonelli.

Gail L. Hunton, *Monmouth County Park System*

Credits:

page xii   (Garden State Parkway), N.J. Turnpike Authority
page 2   (Charles Pike), Monmouth County Planning Board
page 10   (Walter Schoellner), Monmouth County Archives
page 25   (Indian Hill Farm), Randall Gabrielan
page 29   (Deep Cut Farm), Kathy Dorn Severini, DBA Dorn's Classic Images
page 66   (SPUR Benefit), Gerard M. Saydah, Saydah Studios
page 75   (Theodore Narozanick), Monmouth County Archives
page 98   (Helen Herrmann), Lois Pollak Broder and Helen C. Pike
page 129   (Pine Brook Golf Course Dedication), Monmouth County Archives

Acknowledgments

THIS BOOK originated with Jim Truncer's desire to document the accomplishments of the many dedicated people who have contributed to creating and building the Monmouth County Park System in the last six decades. It has been my great pleasure to work with Jim, Gail Hunton, and many other employees and supporters in researching the story of the Park System and summarizing it in this book. All the people I've met along the way share a passion for open space, nature, wildlife and local history, and for helping people enjoy the parks for recreation, learning, and pleasure.

The project began with interviews of twenty-six employees, donors, and elected officials to record their oral histories of the founding and development of the Park System. Gail organized and assisted with the interviews, and Park Ranger Steve Dickinson videotaped most of them. The resulting oral history collection is rich with personal remembrances, insights and details, and it will continue to be a resource for future researchers. We are grateful to all the interviewees for generously sharing their experiences and wisdom. Our interviews with Mike Huber and Ed and Joanne Mullen were particularly inspiring as they graciously related the stories of their major gifts of land to the people of Monmouth County.

Jim's vision and dedication to quality provided inspiration throughout this project. Bruce Gollnick and Dave Compton shared their long perspectives on what it takes to build and operate a first class Park System. Gail, Spence Wickham and Andy Coeyman readily provided access to their Acquisition and Design files during the research, and Faith Hahn articulated her knowledge and vision of planning within the Park System. Joe Sardonia conveyed his knowledge of the design of several park facilities, and Dave Pease relayed his enthusiasm for the game of golf and the exacting maintenance that keeps the Park System's golf courses in top form. Nancy Borchert and Jim Hoffman shared their experience in the administration of the Park System and in building Visitor Services, respectively. Howard Wikoff, Doug Krampert and Tom Kellers all described their experiences in developing historical and nature programs. Ken Thoman and Anna Luiten compiled ecological summaries for the parks that illustrate their intimate knowledge of the natural places, plants and wildlife under the Park System's stewardship.

Research Assistant Daniella Fischetti tirelessly collected and organized historic documents from Park System archives and from the Monmouth County Archives, where Gary Saretzky helped with many requests. Cheryl Stoeber-Goff provided access to numerous documents in the Historical Services archive. Barbara DeLorenzo and Fran Lorelli graciously compiled countless copies of documents for me at Acquisition and Design. Carol Maglio skillfully edited the final manuscript and Frank Mahood significantly enhanced the quality of the book with his excellent designs.

I am especially grateful for the enthusiastic support that Maria Wojciechowski and the Friends of the Parks have provided for several phases of this park history.

Above all, however, I am indebted to Gail Hunton, with whom I've had the pleasure of working on several projects over the last two decades, for her professionalism, grace, and tireless devotion to producing the best book possible with the resources available to us.

Clifford W. Zink

N RECOGNITION of Monmouth County leaders who have actively supported the preservation of open space and the development of outstanding recreational opportunities in Monmouth County.

Monmouth County Board of Chosen Freeholders
1960–2010

Walton Sherman	Thomas J. Powers
Earl L. Woolley	John D'Amico, Jr.
Abram D. Voorhees	Theodore J. Narozanick
Victor E. Grossinger	John A. Villapiano
Joseph C. Irwin	Amy A. Handlin
Charles I. Smith	Carmen M. Stoppiello
Marcus Daly	Edward J. Stominski
Benjamin H. Danskin	Robert D. Clifton
Eugene J. Bedell	William C. Barham
Harry Larrison, Jr.	Lillian G. Burry
Albert E. Allen	Anna C. Little
Axel B. Carlson, Jr.	Barbara J. McMorrow
Ernest G. Kavalek	John P. Curley
Philip N. Gumbs	Amy A. Mallet
Ray Kramer	
Thomas J. Lynch, Jr.	
Jane G. Clayton	
Allan J. MacDonald	
Joseph A. Palaia	
Allan J. Macdonald	
Frank A. Self	
Clement V. Sommers	
Frank A. Campione	

Monmouth County Board of Recreation Commissioners
1962–2010

Victor E. Grossinger	William Kunkel
Walter Schoellner	Paul S. Masnick
James Ackerson	Adeline H. Lubkert
James J. Truncer	Kenneth R. Foulks
Alfred Pool	Nicholas A. Codispoti
Robert Schuchart	Donald M. Lomurro
Donald E. Mc Kelvey	Edward J. Loud
Robert Laughlin	Frederick W. Monsees
Ross W. Maghan	John J. Bradshaw
Chester L. Morgan	Channing P. Irwin
Axel B. Carlson, Jr.	Michael G. Harmon
Albert E. Allen	Nickolas Tuyahov
Ray Kramer	Frederick Kniesler
Craig A. Frankel	Anthony E. Musella
Robert Marks	Fred J. Rummel
Robert M. Higgins	Violeta Peters
Martin J. Vaccaro	Carl Williams, Jr.
Ernest G. Kavalek	N. Britt Raynor
E. Wayne Kavalek	Kevin Mandeville
Allan J. MacDonald	Thomas E. Hennessy, Jr.
James J. O'Shaughnessy	Michael W. Brim
Fyllis G. Feldman	David W. Horsnall
Frank E. Kane	Melvin A. Hood

Part I: The First Fifty Years

Prologue

Construction of the Garden State Parkway in Wall Township, early 1950s.

Superior recreation facilities are an essential component of this environment

IN THE MIDDLE of the 20th century, the postwar economic boom transformed Monmouth County as new roads, jobs, families, and buildings consumed its beautiful farmland, meadows, and forests at an alarming pace. Several farsighted County leaders at that time fortunately saw the need to preserve open space for present and future generations, and they created the Monmouth County Park System in 1960. In its first 50 years the Park System has preserved 16,633 acres, including some of the County's finest natural areas and historic sites, for recreation and conservation.

Many dedicated people have contributed to this accomplishment through their vision, planning, perseverance, commitment to quality, and creative leveraging of County resources with other public resources. Many have also generously donated their land, buildings, artifacts, money, and time. Their collective legacy is one of America's finest county park systems, which will continue to benefit residents and visitors alike for many generations to come.

A sound and orderly development of the County

The construction of the Garden State Parkway in the 1950s provided easy access to shore towns and opened up tens of thousands of acres of prime farmland and forests for development. Between 1940 and 1960 the County's population more than doubled from 161,000 people to 333,000, and nearly half of this growth occurred within three miles of the Parkway. Eighty-five per cent of the population lived along the Bayshore and coast, but demand for new housing and commercial buildings steadily moved inland.

The farsighted business and civic leaders who had grown up in the prewar farming era envisioned a "sound and orderly development of the County," with diverse recreational opportunities and open space as key to ensuring a high quality of life. Their vision drew on the long tradition of public parks in the United States, dating back to Frederick Law Olmstead and Calvert Vaux's efforts a hundred years earlier to create New York's Central Park—the "People's Park"—for recreation and the enjoyment of nature.

The success of Central Park led the New Jersey Legislature in 1894 to authorize counties to develop "ample open spaces for the use of the public." Essex County established the country's first county park commission a year later. With a $2.5 million bond referendum for acquisition and development, Essex County leaders created multiple parks and reservations for recreation and for preserving scenic beauty. Hudson County established a county park commission in 1907, Union County in 1922, Camden County in 1926, and Passaic County in 1927. By 1930, New Jersey's five county park systems had preserved nearly 10,000 acres of prime land, an accomplishment that could not be replicated because of the land's increased value. As wartime development consumed open space in suburban areas, Middlesex, Ocean, and Bergen Counties established park systems in 1940, 1945, and 1946, respectively.

By contrast, the only significant public open spaces in Monmouth County at the end of World War II were Allaire State Park in Howell and Wall Townships, donated by the Arthur Brisbane Estate in 1940, and the State's Turkey Swamp Public Hunting and Fishing Grounds in Freehold Township, established in 1942.

With all the development projects following the Parkway, Joseph C. Irwin, Director of the Monmouth County Board of Chosen Freeholders, saw the need to guide this unprecedented growth. Irwin had served for sixteen years as a Freeholder and two years as Director, and understood political and land use issues around the County. As an avid sportsman and proprietor of the Irwin Yacht Works on the Navesink River in Red Bank, he was also keenly interested in recreation.

Under Irwin's leadership, the Freeholders, including Victor Grossinger, Walton Sherman, Earl L. Woolley, and Abram D. Voorhees, established the Monmouth County Planning Board in April, 1954. They wisely appointed E. Donald Sterner, a Belmar businessman, as Chairman of the Planning Board in July and charged him with establishing "a sound County Planning Program." Sterner had served in the State Assembly and Senate and as the State's first highway commissioner, so he understood the impact of highway construction on suburban and rural areas. He also loved outdoor activities and soon helped to initiate the County's efforts to create parks.

In his first six months as Planning Board Chairman, Sterner organized a county-wide planning conference for officials and residents, set up Agricultural and Resorts and Recreation Committees with dedicated leaders, and hired Charles Pike as the County's first Planning Director. Pike was only 26 years old, but his vision and professionalism provided crucial leadership in the County's nascent planning efforts.

William Duryea, Sterner's pick to head the Agricultural Committee, loved open space and valued its preservation. He served as the sec-

Freeholder Director Joe Irwin, right, at the Howell Park Golf Course dedication with, from left, Recreation Commissioner Axel Carlson, Park System Director Jim Truncer and Governor William Cahill.

JOSEPH C. IRWIN
Mr. Monmouth County

Joseph Irwin's grandfather captained a schooner out of Red Bank that delivered county produce to New York, and young Joe grew up in his family's boat business, the Irwin Yacht Works. He sailed, played football, basketball and baseball, led Red Bank High School's first unbeaten football team in 1922, and played varsity quarterback at Rutgers University. He was elected to the Red Bank Borough Council in 1932 and to the State Assembly in 1936, and served two terms in each post. In 1938 he was elected to the Board of Freeholders where he served for 36 years, 22 of them as Director. He also served for 20 years on the County Planning Board.

Irwin considered the Monmouth County Park System and Brookdale Community College, the county college in Lincroft, his most important accomplishments for Monmouth County residents. When he died in 1987 at the age of 83, State Senator Alfred Beadleston of Rumson said, "He did everything that was within his power to make Monmouth County a better place to live in. The people of this County will be forever in his debt. He was Mr. Monmouth County." Park System Director Jim Truncer remembers Joe often saying, "If it's a choice between politics and the public good, then it's the public good."

CHARLES M. PIKE
Outstanding in planning for the future of Monmouth County

Born in Matawan in 1928, Charles Pike graduated from Rutgers University, where he studied city and regional planning, and later studied at the Columbia University Graduate School of Housing and Planning. After serving in the Korean War as a Marine Captain, he became the County's first Planning Director in 1954 and developed plans for water supply, solid waste, hospitals, and transportation. When he left the Planning Board in 1971 to direct the State's Division of Water Resources, Freeholder Director Irwin told him, "We regret you're leaving us. I think Monmouth County is a better place to live because of Charlie Pike." When Pike died in 1977 at the age of 49, Donald Sterner said, "He was my right arm when we founded the Planning Board," and Irwin commented, "He was a wonderful executive, one of the finest in the state. He was outstanding in planning for the future of Monmouth County."

Swamp' in Freehold Township as a possible County park and also the Earle Naval Air Defense Base in Middletown if the Federal government ever closed it. Schoellner also mentioned a site in Middletown Township that the owner might donate for a County park. In the beginning of their park efforts, County leaders were already looking to leverage County resources with transfers of Federal property and donations.

The three most pressing needs in the County

Charles Pike began studying population, traffic, recreation, land use, and employment in the fall of 1954, "to answer the basic questions of where people live, work, and play and how they travel from place to place, and to help point out deficiencies in existing patterns and indicate future needs." He identified traffic arteries, recreational areas, and protection of surface water supplies as the three most pressing needs and the ones in which the public was most interested.

In his "Survey of Recreational Facilities" in June, 1955, Pike listed municipal parks totaling 132 acres. With only a few parks over 10 acres, he

ond N.J. Secretary of Agriculture from 1925 to 1937 and generously conveyed his farm in Upper Freehold to the State for the Assunpink Wildlife Management Area. In October, 1954, Duryea proposed making Monmouth the 'Best Looking' county in the State by planting along highways, restricting the use of highway frontage, and restoring and creating ponds and lakes for recreation and water conservation.

Sterner responded to Duryea's proposal by raising "the possibility of a County park," and he established the Resort and Recreation Committee with Thomas Heward as its chair and Walter Schoellner as a member to look into it. At their first meeting, they discussed 'Turkey

concluded that "there was a need for a few large parks in the neighborhood of 100 acres to service the populated regions of the county."

Recognizing "the urgency during this time of rapid growth," the Resort and Recreation Committee responded, "The rate of growth of Monmouth County has steadily accelerated during the past few years. To accommodate this growth and also to guarantee a sound and orderly development of the County, the Resort and Recreation Committee recommends that a system of county parks be planned for the dual purpose of conserving the surface water supply of the County and providing additional recreational facilities to the increasing number of year-round residents in the County."

The urgent need of immediate action

The Planning Board adopted the Resort and Recreation Committee's recommendations with a resolution, "realizing the urgent need of immediate action, the Planning Board requests the Board of Freeholders to establish a County Park Commission." Planning Board members and staff identified non-profit corporations, land donations, and referendums as ways to help establish and operate parks. After Morris County voters approved a referendum establishing a County Park Commission in 1956, Thomas Heward told his fellow Planning Board members that "a program linking park areas and water supply would pass a referendum in Monmouth County."

The Freeholders set up a Park Department within the County Planning Board in 1957 and asked the members of the Resorts and Recreation Committee to work on a county parks program for 1957. At the October Planning Board meeting, Donald Sterner "mentioned the possibility that Mrs. Geraldine Thompson might contribute two hundred acres in the Lincroft area for county park purposes (and) stated that within the next month he would like to meet with her to discuss this further." This quiet revelation began an 11-year process that would eventually create Thompson Park, the headquarters of the Park System.

The Freeholders appointed Abram Voorhees as liaison to the Park Department in 1958 and allocated $25,000 for it. Walter Schoellner became chairman of the Resorts and Recreation Committee and sent letters to "all of the local recreation departments and other groups interested in recreation to determine what type of facilities they would be interested in seeing the County develop." He thought that "the most logical approach would be the development of one good centrally-located county park which could serve as a showcase and generate public support."

The Manasquan River, 2006. "The protection of the Manasquan is very important for the County's future," 1955.

Reasons for a County Park System
Resort and Recreation Committee, Monmouth County Planning Board, October 27, 1955

Since the County Planning Board started reviewing subdivisions on January 1, 1955, a total of 93 major subdivisions have been submitted containing 5,190 lots. This represents a total of 2,700 acres or 4.3 square miles. Land is also being swallowed up by highways, business, and industry… As this growth continues westward, much of the open land of the County will be built up and conveniently located park areas will be impossible to obtain.

In a county where land values rest largely upon the availability of attractive open space, it is important to protect our basic assets…Action is needed to keep a portion of the open space, trees, and rural atmosphere which have been one of the chief attractions and economic assets of Monmouth County. Many of our residents commute daily to the metropolitan area and are reminded of the contrast which exists between Monmouth County and those older areas.

County Parks, properly located on the outskirts of heavily developed areas, can be coordinated with zoning, farming, and open tideland uses to define the limits of urban development.

The protection of watersheds, major streams, and dam sites can be accomplished by planning now to protect these areas by incorporation into a county park system. Monmouth County has two major drainage basins and many minor drainage basins which are the major sources of any future surface water supply within the County. The Swimming River is partially developed as a source of potable water; the Manasquan River is entirely undeveloped. The protection of the Manasquan is very important for the County's future.

If the area along these major streams was designated as future Park areas, they could be acquired as development takes place. Along these streams could be located bridle paths, hiking trails, and bicycle trails, and in other areas where adequate access existed and where centers of population are located these could be expanded into major park areas.

A very fine offer

WHEN the N.J. Highway Authority declared 24 acres along the Shark River at the intersection of Tinton Falls and Wall and Neptune Townships as surplus property left over from the Parkway, County leaders thought the site, which included part of a former Girl Scout Camp with woods and wetlands, would make a fine county park. In February, 1960, the Freeholders agreed to match a $15,000 bid that the Highway Authority had received for the land, and in March Neptune Township Committee members offered to donate five adjacent acres to the park, which Joe Irwin called a "very fine offer." Neptune officials ultimately donated 40 acres to Shark River Park, the first of many land donations to the Park System.

The acquisition of the Shark River site for the first county park in May, 1960 marked the beginning of the County's park system. In 1960, Monmouth was way behind other central New Jersey counties. Ocean had 250 acres of parkland for its 96,000 people; Mercer had 623 acres for 266,000 people; Somerset had 800 acres for 143,000 people; Middlesex had 1,080 acres for 432,000 people; and Morris had 2,200 acres for 260,000 people. Monmouth County had one 24-acre park for its 334,000 residents.

Planning Director Pike developed a comprehensive plan for year-round use of Shark River Park, with a pond for fishing and skating, picnic tables and grills, a playground and playfields, a shelter building, restrooms, parking, and trails. He enlisted the Freehold Soil Conserva-

tion District to dig the pond, the County Engineer's Office to provide the engineering, the County Road Department to provide employees and equipment, and the Corrections Department to provide prisoners for some of the labor. Crews started working on June 22, 1960, about three weeks after the County took possession of the site. With Shark River Park, Pike and other county officials established the precedent for high quality recreational facilities and for maximizing the County's investment with additional resources.

The urgency of the problem cannot be overemphasized

After getting Shark River Park underway, Pike used a grant from the Federal Housing and Home Finance Agency to produce a "Recreation Study and Plan" in December, 1960, that laid out a blueprint for establishing the County's park system on a "firm foundation" of facts and careful planning. In this remarkably prescient study, Pike wrote,

Higher incomes, a shorter work week, paid vacations and holidays, earlier retirement, and longer life spans, are a few of the major factors which have led to the need for increased opportunities for leisure time activities. In addition to these national changes affecting recreation in all areas of the country, the need is further actuated in Monmouth County and the Monmouth Coastal Region by a rapid expansion of population and the transition in the character of the region. The outward pressure from the New York - North Jersey Metropolitan area will continue to result in a growing

Left: Construction of the pond at Shark River Park, 1961.

Right: Ice skating on the pond at Shark River Park, 1968. Shark River Park opened in 1961 and was immediately popular, with over 5,900 visitors during its first year.

Opposite page: Shark River Park.

population and a corollary diminution in farms, open space and woodland.

Monmouth County has long been known as a recreational center with its beaches and waterways drawing summer visitors from great distances. The recreational opportunities in recent years have also attracted many permanent residents seeking an ideal environment. The municipalities of the region are planning for a high type of residential and industrial development. There is severe competition for this selective type of development which is extremely

sensitive to the environment in which it locates. Superior recreation facilities are an essential component of this environment. To preserve the natural recreation advantages of the County and attract the desired type of development cannot be left to chance. It will require careful planning with foresight followed by determined action. The region and County must keep pace with growth and development by expanding recreational opportunities.

Pike proposed creating regional county parks for current and future recreation, conservation of natural areas and wildlife, protection of water supplies, preservation of rural landscape aesthetics, and the limitation of intensive development. For a "comprehensive system of reserving open space," he proposed both "the outright purchase of strategically located open areas" and "conservation easements…which would limit a property to agricultural and other open uses." As he noted, "The benefits to the public are many and varied and accrue not only to the present population in surrounding developed areas but to future generations."

Recommending that "County parks should be nature oriented and accentuate facilities which cannot be economically or efficiently developed and maintained by municipalities," Charles Pike called for "an equitable distribution of facilities" to serve people throughout the County. Anticipating that some private recreation facilities like golf courses would be lost to development, he foresaw the need for "public replacement to guarantee well-rounded and diversified regional recreational facilities."

Noting that acquisition opportunities east of the Parkway were rapidly fading, he stressed, "The urgency of the problem cannot be overemphasized. The key to a good County Park system for Monmouth is immediate acquisition of land in the path of continuing development taking place westward from the coast."

Pike recommended acquiring land adjacent to Shark River Park "to realize the full potential of this site," along the Swimming River to protect its watershed, along the Manasquan River for "the development of surface water supply," at bayshore and ocean beaches, and in the County's "Western Area" to meet the "growing needs" there. With the State's Division of Water Policy and Supply considering a 3.8 billion gallon off-stream reservoir to capture Manasquan River water for public consumption, he recommended that "the Manasquan be developed for multiple uses with full utilization of its recreational potential." His vision for fishing, hiking, and boating at the reservoir would eventually lead to one of the County's most visited parks, the Manasquan Reservoir.

In calling for "superior recreational facilities" providing a range of activities near population centers and for preserving open space for watershed and wildlife protection and the enjoyment of nature, the "Recreation Study and Plan" provided the blueprint for developing the Monmouth County Park System.

The Freeholders appropriated $75,000 for the Department of Parks in 1961 to finish Shark River Park and, after it opened in May, the high number of visitors quickly demonstrated the demand for year-round regional recreation facilities in Monmouth. The County's planning efforts proved to be quite timely that year, as Governor Robert B. Meyner proposed the State's first Green Acres Bond Act of $60 million to double the amount of State land from 250,000 to 500,000 acres and to support local land preservation with matching grants. At their June meeting, the members of the Planning Board resolved to "develop existing recommendations for County parks to the point where the County can take advantage of funds to be supplied for the 'Green Acres' program if it passes the November referendum."

We've got to live with nature

While County leaders worked on plans to acquire land for parks, Mrs. Geraldine L. Thompson invited Freeholder Director Joseph Irwin in the fall of 1961 to discuss her interest in donating Brookdale Farm in Lincroft for a County park. Mrs. Thompson had lived on Brookdale Farm, one of New Jersey's premier horse estates, since 1896 and she often welcomed children and families to enjoy its natural beauty. In the late 1950s, she told a reporter, "We've got to live with nature. The children have to feel the ground beneath them and go out in the woods and see the trees and birds." After her meeting with Irwin, she told another reporter, "I would like nothing better than to know that Brookdale in the future would be an open place for children and for animals because they have a place here, too… I would want it to be under the control of the county and open to all."

Irwin followed up the meeting by writing to her, "Brookdale Farm has probably the greatest potential for County Park development of any lands in the County… We are most gratified that you are giving this matter serious consideration…The Park Department and Board of Freeholders recognize a critical need for the preservation of a County Park area in the northern part of the County, which is growing more rapidly than any other. We have been investigating a number of sites, none of which have the outstanding potential of Brookdale Farm."

Geraldine Thompson, owner of Brookdale Farm, in the 1950s. During her long lifetime, she worked to improve the early public health, welfare, and juvenile justice programs in the County and State, and was known to many of her contemporaries as the "First Lady of New Jersey."

After New Jersey voters overwhelmingly approved the $60 million Green Acres Bond Act in November, 1961, Joseph Irwin and Donald Sterner quickly met with Matthew Adams, Commissioner of the State's Department of Conservation and Economic Development, to discuss the County's park plans. Assemblyman Alfred Beadleston wrote to Commissioner Adams on December 8th that "Monmouth County is extremely anxious to share in the Green Acres program…The Monmouth County Board of Freeholders and the Planning Board have done a fine job in planning for these recreational areas, and I sincerely believe that your Department should do everything possible to cooperate fully in making realities of their proposals."

In a County meeting with Holmdel officials in early 1962 to discuss potential sites, William (Jay) Duncan, who was the secretary of the Holmdel Planning Board, offered to sell his farm to the County for a park. Charles Pike and his colleagues were delighted, as Duncan's 137-acre farm—historically known as Longstreet Farm—was ideally located in a populated area and large enough for a regional park, and it was also one of the County's most historic farms. Mary Holmes Duncan, Jay Duncan's wife, was born on the farm and was a descendent of the

original Longstreet settlers. Since the Green Acres regulations did not permit the purchase of improvements, Pike excluded the 6-acre Longstreet homestead from the purchase, but indicated that the County would like to acquire it later on.

Planning Director Pike and his staff identified another potential park site in Freehold Township next to the State's Turkey Swamp Public Hunting and Fishing Grounds. Containing both pinelands and upland forest, the 189-acre Bohnke Farm and the adjacent 83-acre Schnitzler property on Georgia Tavern Road offered the potential for both recreation and the conservation of important natural areas.

To take advantage of these opportunities, Monmouth officials pre-

View of Longstreet Farm in 1974. When Green Acres changed its regulations in 1965 to permit the acquisition of properties with "improvements," park officials negotiated a purchase agreement allowing Mr. and Mrs. Duncan to live in the farmhouse at Longstreet Farm for the rest of their lives while the Park System restored the farm's outbuildings and opened them to the public.

pared the County's first Green Acres applications in 1962 to acquire the three farms to establish Holmdel and Turkey Swamp Parks.

A uniformly high standard of recreational activities

After submitting the Green Acres applications, Joseph Irwin and his fellow Freeholders created the Board of Recreation Commissioners, as provided for in State legislation, to run the County parks. In August, 1962, they appointed the three-member Board, with Victor E. Grossinger as Chairman and James Ackerson and Walter Schoellner as members, to promote "a uniformly high standard of recreational activities throughout the County."

Victor Grossinger lived in Middletown and knew the County well. He had grown up on a horse farm, was a partner in Grossinger and Heller, a real estate and insurance firm in Red Bank, and had served four terms on the Board of Freeholders. Walter Schoellner was a retired businessman who lived in Middletown and loved the outdoors. He had served on the County Planning Board's Resort and Recreation Committee since 1955, and he had worked closely with Charles Pike and Donald Sterner in examining potential park sites and in setting up Shark River Park. Jim Ackerson grew up and farmed in Holmdel and was the Mayor of Holmdel.

Green Acres awarded the County matching grants in the fall of 1962 to establish Holmdel and Turkey Swamp Parks. At the Freeholders'

Victor Grossinger (right) with Park System naturalist Tom Kellers in 1975

VICTOR E. GROSSINGER, *A fine gentleman*

Victor Grossinger, or "Bud" as everyone called him, grew up in Middletown on Indian Springs Farm, which is now Tatum Park. His father ran the farm for Charles Tatum, and Bud worked closely with Tatum's daughter-in-law, Genevieve Tatum, in securing her donation of the farm to the County in 1973.

Grossinger grew up cherishing the "rolling countryside of the County," and remembered when wagons loaded with hay, corn, and potatoes from Monmouth farms lined up to be loaded onto steamers at Keyport and Red Bank for the trip to New York. As he recalled, "During that pastoral period, an open field meant work, not play…A kid's day off meant taking a horse to the blacksmith. There wasn't a place where you could stop and enjoy more than an arm's length of room."

Victor Grossinger served on the Middletown Township Committee from 1932 to 1944, when the Freeholders appointed him to fill a vacancy on their Board where he served four terms. He served as the first Chairman of the Board of Recreation Commissioners from 1962 until his death in 1980 and oversaw the growth of the Park System to over 4,000 acres in 17 parks with 185 employees. Commissioner Grossinger was most proud of Longstreet Farm and its interpretation of turn-of-the-century farming, "When you go through the farm there it makes you appreciate how hard farmers worked." The National Association of Counties recognized his contributions with its Park and Recreation Officials Award in 1978.

Left: Work on Holmdel Park's roads and main pond began in 1963, and the park opened in May of the following year.

Right: Holmdel Park's ever-popular sledding hill opened in 1968 and is pictured here in 1977.

organizational meeting in January, 1963, Freeholder Director Irwin said that these new parks "will be a great asset to the people of Monmouth County and during the coming years will be enjoyed by hundreds of thousands." The Recreation Commissioners appointed Walter Schoellner as Director of Parks, "to stimulate the full utilization of park and recreational facilities," and Charles Pike provided him a desk and clerical support in the Planning Board office on Court Street in Freehold.

To maximize the County's park efforts, Charles Pike suggested to Walter Schoellner and the Freeholders that they hire a person with parks training and experience. Pike recommended Jim Truncer, an Allentown resident who was a State Park superintendent working with the Green Acres program in the State Parks Land Office in Trenton. Jim was "born into the business" of parks and recreation, as he later said,

WALTER SCHOELLNER

A natural choice

Walter Schoellner was born in Newark but had spent summers in Leonardo since he was a small child and moved there in 1925. He served as a lieutenant commander in the U.S. Coast Guard Auxiliary in Atlantic Highlands during the Second World War and served as Chief Harbor Master there until 1960.

Over the years Schoellner hunted and fished in many parts of the County, "walking fields and woodlands and becoming quite familiar with the variety of trees, wildflowers, and wildlife in the region." He served eight years on the County Planning Board, helped establish Shark River Park, and was a member of the County Shade Tree Commission.

Walter was a "natural choice" to run the Board of Recreation Commissioners in 1962, and he served as Board Secretary from 1964 to 1967. He championed the preservation of Hartshorne Woods and worked to create Howell Park, the site of the County's first golf course.

having grown up in Parvin State Park where his father, Joseph Truncer, was Superintendent. Following Freeholder Benjamin Danskin's advice, the Freeholders appointed Jim in August of 1963 to the Recreation Commission so that he could learn about County operations and staff.

If and when this land is available

As Charles Pike and Walter Schoellner worked on Holmdel Park in 1963, they were already thinking of expanding it. In 1955, the U.S. Army had installed Nike Battery 54, including a 22-acre Control Area in Holmdel Township, as part of its Cold War defenses for New York City, but it was already becoming obsolete. Schoellner wrote in December to Albert Wilson, chief of the U.S. General Services Administration's Real Property Division, "We would appreciate hearing from you if and when this land is available, as we believe the County of Monmouth would be interested in acquiring this piece of land to add to its Park holdings which join this Base." While Wilson responded that the Nike Base remained active, County officials had planted the seed to acquire it.

In June, 1964, Charles Pike hired Jim Truncer as the first parks professional on the County staff and he stepped down from the Board of Recreation Commissioners. As Jim recalled,

> I was hired as a principal park planner on the Planning Board payroll, after I spent just under a year on the Recreation Commission. There were probably no more than 10 employees when I got here. There were three or four at Shark River, three or four at Holmdel, and two down at Turkey Swamp. Some were on the road department payroll, as one gentleman had been a foreman with the road department. Another had worked in buildings and grounds. They were still on the other department payrolls. When I started there were three of us working in a 12 ft. by 14 ft. room on the third floor of the Hall of Records—my desk was a drafting table; Walter Schoellner, who was Secretary to the Board, had a desk, and so did Mrs. Florence Murphy, the secretary. So, we were used to being close to one another.

Jim put together a budget for 1965 that included seventeen full-time and six summer employees, as well as a five-year outline of capital improvements, including the acquisition of at least 500 acres "to raise the County Park areas to the minimum standards required." The Freeholders requested that Jim look for sites "eligible for Green Acre funds before the program expires," and he proposed doubling the size of Holmdel Park to over 300 acres, primarily "to provide protection of the existing stream courses which flow through the area." When a Holmdel official asked Charles Pike if there was a need for the additional acreage, he responded,

There is no doubt about it. The County is somewhat behind counties of a similar character. We have tried to plan a park system so that these parks would serve an area of the County, and to make them large facilities, as opposed to local active recreation. The primary purpose of the County Park is to preserve land in its natural state. As time goes on, this will draw people outside the township and will serve the Bayshore area or the north section of the County. That will be the function of the park.

Great possibilities for recreation

In early 1965 County leaders set their sights on another Federal site destined to become surplus property. The U.S. Army was starting to decommission part of its 250-acre Highlands Army Air Defense Site (H.A.A.D.S.) that adjoined forested highlands known as Hartshorne Woods, property the Hartshorne family had owned since Richard Hartshorne first settled the area in the 1680s. Walter Schoellner wanted to preserve Hartshorne Woods, and he wrote to the U.S. General Services Administration to express the County's interest in the adjacent H.A.A.D.S. parcel as well.

Walter also wrote to Clifford P. Case, New Jersey's senior senator, seeking his help, "We are vitally interested in the acquisition of desirable land areas. This 103-acre piece not only affords historic value as the first promontory you see when approaching New York harbor from the sea, but parts of this area are still untouched and, as natural areas, could be preserved for posterity. As this land area is bordered on two sides by the Navesink and Shrewsbury Rivers, it will afford great possibilities for recreation." County officials would tenaciously work to preserve the entire H.A.A.D.S. property over the next 20 years.

With visitation growing at the County's three parks, the Recreation Commissioners adopted a County Park and Recreation Policy in 1965 "to preserve the beauty of the parks; to protect the wildlife that adds to the interest of the park; to maintain peace, quiet, and respectability so that the county parks and recreation areas can be enjoyed by those who come with the serious intent to enjoy them; and to maintain as high a standard as possible in serving the public and to protect visitors from impositions."

The Board of Recreation Commissioners in the early 1970s. Standing are Freeholder Buddy Allen, Jim Truncer, and Robert Laughlin. Seated are Ross Maghan, Victor Grossinger, and Donald McKelvey.

JAMES J. TRUNCER, Secretary-Director
Monmouth County Park System

Parvin State Park was my backyard

My father was born in Williamstown in Gloucester County, and he was trained as a forester at the New York State College School of Forestry at Syracuse University. He wound up working for the State of New Jersey as a land surveyor and, as the first Superintendent at Parvin State Park, he was involved in its development and then ran it.

My mother and dad would often take their canoe up the head waters of the lake, and we'd stop somewhere along the way and bathe or have a picnic lunch as a family activity. In summers there were lots of people boating, swimming, fishing. In winters we walked out across the frozen lake, and my dad would take a hatchet and go test the ice to see how thick it was. In terms of experiences growing up, living there, I had just a myriad of them. So, Parvin State Park was my backyard.

I hung around the park and the work crews and went with them, and went around with my dad. In his philosophy he was service oriented, in terms of people having worthwhile, enjoyable experi-

ences. One of the things I always admired about my father was his work ethic...I think we're ultimately judged by the work that we produce and how well we do it, the quality of the work. While some people may get ahead faster, in the final analysis, I learned that it's the quality of the work that stands out and separates you.

Jim earned a bachelor's degree in park management and resource development at Michigan State University in 1961 and worked as a planner for the National Park Service's regional office in Virginia. After serving on active duty in the N.J. Air National Guard, he went to work for the State Parks Lands Office and Green Acres Land Acquisition projects. The Freeholders appointed him to the Board of Recreation Commissioners in 1963, and after he earned a master's degree in park and recreation administration from Michigan State in 1964, he left the Board and became the Director of County Parks and Recreation in 1966. In 1974 he became the Board Secretary and continues to serve in that position.

In the first of several revisions over the years, the Recreation Commissioners updated their Park and Recreation Policy in 1968 to preserve "examples of nature's handiwork for the appreciation and enjoyment of this and future generations, while maintaining the surroundings as a naturalistic setting without obtrusive evidence of man's interference. The natural beauty spots embraced within the Monmouth County Parks are a great natural resource belonging to the people that should be protected and preserved for all time."

As more people moved into the County, there was a growing interest in golf, which Eatontown realtor Harold Lindemann knew well from his clients. Lindemann recommended in 1965 that the County purchase the 302-acre Windsor Stock Farm along the Manasquan River in Howell Township for a golf course, writing to Walter Schoellner,

It is a rare property and it would be hard to find such a large tract in Monmouth County which has the combination of being on the river, having a good brook, numerous ponds in such a natural untouched setting, and a group of buildings on a knoll in such good condition. It would seem that this property would be ideal for a golf course combined with recreational areas in the wooded portions...At the rate developers are buying land, such places will be nonexistent for County purposes in a few years or, if available, will be priced out of reach for use as golf courses.

The Highlands Army Air Defense Site (H.A.A.D.S.) about 1985, prior to demolition of the military structures.

A continuing governmental responsibility

County Park and Recreation Policy for Monmouth County Board of Recreation Commissioners, 1965

Recreation is truly the improvement process necessary for the continued refreshment of the body and mind throughout the lifetime of the individual. Recreation is a human need, contributing to human happiness, and essential to the well-being of people and, as such, the public welfare is promoted by providing opportunities for wholesome and adequate recreation.

The nurturing of human resources is more important to the full economic potential of this County and to the State and Nation than any materialistic ethic. The development of human resources is inescapably related to recreation and education: eliminating ignorance, preparation for the fruitful use of leisure to improve the quality of living, and providing for an advanced technology society based on pride in work and earned leisure.

Recreation is a legitimate, continuing governmental responsibility directly associated with the public welfare. As such, the adequacy, quality, and continuity of the Park and recreation programs and opportunities provided at all governmental levels should be supported and advanced by professional leadership through the use of public and other supplemental funds.

Freeholders Joseph Irwin and Benjamin Danskin were very interested but concerned about the challenges of developing and operating a golf course. As Jim Truncer recalled, "Joe basically said to me, 'What do you think? Do you think we can do this?' And I said, 'Yes, if that's what the Board would like to do, I see no reason why we can't. We would have to hire a golf course architect to look at it.'"

The Freeholders purchased the Windsor Stock Farm in 1967 with a matching Green Acres grant and an additional grant from U.S. Department of Housing and Urban Development's Open Space Fund. The Recreation Commissioners named the new site the Howell Park Golf Course, and they commissioned the noted golf course architect Francis Duane to design it. The Commissioners and Park System staff had to learn how to build and operate a golf course.

In March, 1966, the Freeholders appointed Jim Truncer as the Director of County Parks and Recreation. They also appointed Harry Larrison

Harry Larrison, right, 1981.

HARRY LARRISON

There's nothing more rewarding than helping people

Harry Larrison was born in Neptune and played All State football and basketball in high school. When he graduated he moved to Ocean Grove to pick up and deliver coal for his grandfather, John Larrison, who owned Larrison Coal and Oil Company. As Harry later recalled,

When you travel, you take note of places where there's no open space, and I just made up my mind that we had to do something in Monmouth County to be sure that we preserved as much as we can…I think we all realized we had to do something to protect the land, so we just wanted an ambitious plan to buy parks.

Harry joined the Eagle Hook and Ladder Fire Company, where his grandfather was a member, and the Ocean Grove First Aid Squad and served in both of these organizations for over 50 years. Harry was elected twice to the Neptune Township Committee and nine times to the Board of Freeholders, where he served as Director for 22 years. Regarding his years of public service, Larrison said, "I love the county. I really do. And I love the people in it. People are what make life worthwhile. I think there's nothing more rewarding than helping people." After he died in 2005 at the age of 79, Freeholder Director Thomas Powers, who ran with him in eight campaigns, said, "Harry was involved in everything good this county accomplished for the past 40 years."

of Ocean Grove to fill a vacant seat on the Board of Freeholders, and he quickly became a major booster of preserving open space in the County. In nearly four decades of public service as a Freeholder, Larrison always supported the Park System's efforts, and often played a key role in preserving specific parcels of land for County parks.

It was a great time

As visitation in the four County parks approached 100,000 in 1965, nature walks led by Tom Kellers proved to be especially popular. Jim Truncer had hired Tom at the recommendation of Dave Moore, the Superintendent of Allaire State Park, where Tom also led nature walks.

The Windsor Stock Farm in 1967, future site of the Howell Park Golf Course.

Kellers had grown up on his family's farm in Wall Township where they bred pigs and sold corn and tomatoes from a roadside stand. He thought that he would be a farmer himself but, after graduating from Cook College at Rutgers University in 1960, he studied biochemistry and animal nutrition in graduate school and earned an education degree. Tom was teaching middle school science in 1964 when Dave asked him to lead some nature walks at Allaire State Park.

Jim hired Tom Kellers as the Park System's first full-time naturalist in 1966, and he joined the administrative staff in its cramped office on South Street in Freehold. As Tom recalled, "We were always having discussions about developing programs and activities for the parks. We thought that if people are going to see these resources as valuable, we had to get them to enjoy the parks and appreciate them. We would feed ideas off of each other. It was a great time." "We never said no," Jim recalled, "There wasn't anything we couldn't do. When someone would call and ask if we had a program, we would put one together."

Tom recalled that in the fall of 1966, "Jim thought it would be a good idea to put together a monthly newsletter about what we were doing in the parks, and I volunteered to do it. I wrote the text, Florence Murphy and Judy Zurick typed it up on an IBM and justified it, and then I put together the mechanicals." They produced the first *Green Heritage* in January of 1967, and the Park System continues to publish the popular newsletter quarterly.

Archery program at Turkey Swamp Park, 1960s.

Turkey Swamp Park opened in 1966 with a 20-acre lake, family campgrounds, and trails through the pine woods. This rustic style shelter building, still in use, was built overlooking the lake.

When the County acquired the 6-acre Longstreet farmstead at Holmdel Park in 1967, Tom Kellers and Jim Truncer consulted with members of the County's Agricultural Committee and decided to interpret the farm to the 1890s, "when agricultural technology was shifting from horses to tractors." As Tom recalled, "barn doors opened up all over the county," and farmers contributed old equipment and tools they had been saving for decades. The *Asbury Park Press* soon reported,

An old Holmdel Farm is being transformed by the County Park System into a living replica of Monmouth County's agricultural past. The Duncan farm will be run by Park employees using authentic old farm machinery from before the age of mechanization. The farm, according to naturalist K. T. Kellers, will serve as an illustration to county residents and visitors of what farming used to be like in Monmouth County. The department is now collecting old equipment to be used on the farm. Most of the pieces acquired so far date back to the turn of the century, with some going back to 1870.

In the summer of 1967 Jim hired the first of several young people who have played key roles in the development of the Park System and continue to do so. Bruce Gollnick became a seasonal employee for the first of two summers at Turkey Swamp Park. He had grown up in New Egypt, graduated from Allentown High School, and was study-ing forestry at Lassen College in California. As Jim recalled, "We had a conversation about careers and he was thinking of forestry. I said, 'You ought to think about parks. Forestry is not a growing profession and I think there would be more opportunities in parks.'"

Bruce took Jim's advice and finished at North Carolina State in the resource department, which included parks and recreation, and for-estry and wildlife management. Bruce's decision to follow this career path has proven enormously beneficial to the Park System over the last four decades.

In the summer of 1968 Jim Truncer hired Spencer Wickham, who had just graduated as a landscape architect from Cook College at Rutgers University, to help design park improvements. Spence started surveying Brookdale Farm that fall, but he was drafted in January, 1969, for service in Vietnam. After returning for a tour of duty at Fort Dix, Jim told him, "When you get out, you have your old job back." Spence rejoined the Park System staff in 1971, and became head of the Acquisi-tion and Design Department in 1976.

Solely for park purposes

When Geraldine L. Thompson passed away at the age of 95 in Sep-tember of 1967, she bequeathed 215 acres of Brookdale Farm "together with the buildings and improvements thereon… to the Board of Chosen Freeholders of Monmouth County… to be used in perpetuity solely for park purposes." Mrs. Thompson's donation included her mag-nificent residence, large barns and stables, paddocks, several houses and maintenance buildings. She provided a year of additional employ-ment for her staff, giving Jim and his staff time to develop a park plan for the site. Her generous donation created Thompson Park as the centerpiece of Monmouth County's Park System.

A deep concern for open space

Geraldine Thompson's donation of Brookdale Farm for Thompson Park and the growing success of the Park System inspired two other Monmouth County women to donate their farms, located within one and a half miles of each other in Freehold Township, in 1969. Like Mrs. Thompson, Jim Truncer noted, "The two donors had a deep concern for open space and wanted to see their lands preserved and not subdi-vided and developed."

BRUCE GOLLNICK
Assistant Director
Monmouth County
Park System

*Enormously
beneficial to the
Park System*

Bruce Gollnick was born in New Egypt but went to high school in Allentown where his father ran a family business. His mother's family had a feed mill in Cookstown and a dairy farm near Jacob-stown, and he remembers "always being interested in history and archaeology."

When he went to work in Turkey Swamp Park in the summer of 1967, Bruce's assignment was "to maintain the facility and take care of the public." He returned to Turkey Swamp the follow-ing summer, and today it remains his favorite park because of its "primitiveness." In the summer of 1969 he worked as an intern at Holmdel and Shark River Parks in Special Maintenance. Bruce served an internship at the Northern Virginia Regional Park Authority in the summer of 1970 as he recalled, "to benefit from some experience elsewhere." When he returned to the Park Sys-tem full time in January of 1971 at the age of 22, Jim named him Assistant Superintendent of Parks, and he has served as Assistant Director since 1984.

Thompson Park in the 1970s with all the grand estate features—stately trees, expansive pastures, and handsome buildings—that made Brookdale Farm a superior setting for a County park.

SPENCER WICKHAM
Chief of Acquisition
and Design

The best of both worlds

Spence Wickham developed a love of the outdoors while visiting and working at his grandparents' potato farm on the north shore of Long Island. Spence's family had moved from Long Island to Everett, about a mile north of Brookdale Farm, when he was 11. As he recalled,

We used to come down to Brookdale Farm in the winter and skate on a little pond behind one of the residences off the mainte-nance yard. There was always a bonfire going and Mrs. Thompson never had a problem. She enjoyed the company of the kids. She was very down-to-earth, very hospitable.

Spence planned to study agricultural engineering at Cook Col-lege but switched to landscape architecture, as he recalled,

This business of designing a landscape and then going out and actually installing it seemed to be kind of exciting and the best of both worlds; being able to do some design work and then trans-ferring that to the ground and, hopefully, having a happy client. I enjoyed it.

Helen Hermann of West Long Branch donated 35 acres of Baysholm, her 76-acre farm on Burlington Road in Freehold Township. Ms. Her-mann first came to Monmouth County as a young girl, spending her summer vacations at her family's home in Elberon in the south part of Long Branch. She bought the William Henry Wikoff Farm in 1946, renamed it Baysholm, an old English word for 'young calves meadow,' and ran it for 24 years. The Recreation Commissioners named the site the Baysholm Conservation Area. She donated an additional 36 acres to it in 1973. Elizabeth Durand donated 90 acres of her farm on Ran-dolph Road in Freehold Township, including fields, woods, marshes,

and a 3½-acre pond, and the Recreation Commissioners named it the Durand Conservation Area.

To highlight progress from the opening of Shark River Park in 1961 to preserving nearly 2,000 acres in five parks, Park System staff produced a 1968 Annual Report. This first Annual Report recognized the contri-butions of eighteen individuals and groups as "Friends of Monmouth County Parks," and highlighted the County's success in "fully utilizing" grants from Federal and State agencies "to protect open spaces that are vitally needed for the public good." In the Report the staff noted, "It is well that our land acquisitions have moved ahead in 1968. The urban sprawl has created a burgeoning population and a condition where open spaces and lands of high recreational value are being purchased and restructured at an alarmingly rapid rate."

During the 1960s the overall County population grew by 38%. From 1960 to 1969, the number of farms in the County fell 45% from 1412 to 783. In the 1969 Annual Report, Park System staff noted, "The preserva-tion of open space is one of the most critical environmental needs of our time…Open farm lands in our county are disappearing at a rate in excess of 2,500 acres a year, with new homes and structures occupy-ing what was once an open field and woodlot." In its first decade, the Park System had preserved, with the help of Green Acres grants and generous donations, 1,635 acres, created seven parks, and welcomed 1.2 million visitors.

The permanent legacy we leave to our future generations

Monmouth County Park System Annual Report 1968

To the Citizens of Monmouth County:

We have been most fortunate in being able to acquire and set aside some of Monmouth County's most valuable and scenic lands for the enjoyment of our county's citizens. The accomplishments as shown in this report could only have been realized as a result of the Board of Chosen Freeholders' interest and dedication in providing an outstand-ing countywide park and recreation system.

The goal of the Monmouth County Board of Recreation Commissioners has been and will

continue to be a program of providing the great-est possible benefits for the greatest number of citizens over the longest possible period of time. Members of our Board are dedicated to serving the public and are consistently guided by their realization that what is preserved today will become a part of the permanent legacy we leave to our future generations.

Victor E. Grossinger, Chairman
Board of Recreation Commissioners

N PREPARATION for the Park System's second decade, Jim Truncer and Tom Kellers prepared the "Monmouth County Open Space Plan 1970-1985," with emphasis on preserving natural areas, particularly along streams, and developing new recreation opportunities. Citing annual attendance growth at the County parks from 8,800 in 1962 to nearly 595,000 in 1970, including a remarkable 44% increase in 1970, the "Open Space Plan" noted,

The figures show that new park sites only awaken a latent interest in participating in outdoor activities, causing the total attendance figures to rise even higher. This is a good indication that present facilities are not sufficient to meet the present demand... As citizens become more sophisticated in their discretionary time activities and as older citizens become more active, the spectrum of recreation opportunities will have to be expanded.

The "Open Space Plan" proposed several ways to expand the County's indoor and outdoor recreation opportunities, including regional recreation centers with flexible facilities for multiple activities, from sports to crafts to theatre. The plan also proposed a network of bikeways and trails linking parks and towns in many parts of the County and greenways protecting stream corridors. All of these recommendations would become key and popular components of the Park System over the next four decades.

Park staff targeted five areas for new County parks in the "Open Space Plan": Upper Freehold Township near Imlaystown, Millstone Township near Perrineville Lake, Marlboro Township near Big Brook, Hartshorne Woods and the H.A.A.D.S. parcel in Middletown Town-

ship, and Ocean Township near Cranberry Brook. The plan was timely, as voters approved the second Green Acres Bond Act in 1971 for $80 million of open space funding. The Freeholders would establish new County parks in each of the targeted areas and in several others, but the "competition for land" that the "Open Space Plan" predicted for the 1970s would require multi-year efforts to establish most of them.

Recognizing that "Government agencies have a most definite need for land purchase programs designed to move as rapidly as their competitors," the "Open Space Plan" identified several strategies that have proved to be especially important in the growth of the Park System. To finance purchases when timing is critical, the "Open Space Plan" recommended establishing "a land bank revolving fund so that land purchases by government may move as rapidly as private enterprise." The N.J. Conservation Foundation initially provided this critical assistance to the Park System, followed by the Monmouth Conservation Foundation.

The plan suggested consideration of an open space tax to provide a dedicated funding source for land preservation and recreation facilities. Monmouth County would lead the state in establishing this critical program in the 1980s. The plan also recommended preserving open space and protecting historic and natural resources through purchases or donations of easements on private property. The Park System used easements to preserve nearly 2,000 acres by the end of 2009.

The "Open Space Plan" also recommended transfers of government property to preserve publicly-owned sites. The Freeholders purchased 160 acres on Kozloski Road in Freehold Township for a new administrative complex in 1970, but did not need the whole site, and they transferred 61 acres to the Park System for recreational use. Because of its central location, Park System staff soon established East Freehold Park as the location of the popular Monmouth County Fair.

There's no excuse for anyone

In early 1970 the Park System staff moved from Freehold to offices in Thompson Park in the former summer home of Dr. William Payne Thompson, which became the Park System's Administrative Headquarters. To coordinate and expand recreation activities and interpretive nature programs, Park System officials created the Visitor Services Department in the former Thompson House in 1971. Tom Kellers became the head of Visitor Services and hired Bob Henschel as a park naturalist. They and their staff set up nature exhibits in the house, which soon

Local newspapers such as the *Red Bank Register* and the *Asbury Park Press* provided important editorial support for the County's open space preservation program. *Red Bank Register*, September 2, 1971.

Monmouth County Park System Annual Report 1970

1970 was a year in which the people of Monmouth County developed a new sense of environmental awareness. They became concerned and involved with the problems of wildlife preservation, pollution, and conservation of natural resources. A 44% increase in the number of County Park visitors during 1970 reflects a new ecological conscience and an attempt by our citizens to utilize their natural resources to the fullest extent.

Opposite page: Weltz Park.

Left: Cross-country runners in Holmdel Park, 1979. Statewide cross-country meets bring thousands of athletes and onlookers to Holmdel Park each fall.

Right: Children's Theater in Thompson Park, 1972. One of Thompson Park's spacious horse barns became the home for the Park System's summer theater productions in 1982.

became known as the Thompson Park Visitor Center. They developed programs that used the parks as "outdoor classrooms" to teach children and adults about local plants and animals.

Visitor Services staff also developed free "Recreation Clinics" to help visitors learn basic skills for activities like cross country skiing, horse care, archery, hiking, and fishing. In the summer, they organized "Fun in the Sun" with canoeing, hiking, swimming, and field sports. For visitors interested in cultural activities, the staff created art and drama programs at the Visitor Center. In their first year, Visitor Services employees presented 1,600 interpretive programs to 46,000 people.

Visitor Services staff soon created a "Special Skills" program with activities like backpacking and survival, horseback riding and horse care, bicycle touring, canoeing, fly-tying and fishing, early American crafts, ceramics, taxidermy, flower arranging, landscaping, golf, pottery, sailing, and tennis. Park naturalists led campfire programs, bird watching, live snake demonstrations, nature photography, and nature hikes. Other staff oversaw Opera in the Park—*La Boheme*—at the Thompson Park theater barn, as well as turtle races, horseshoe and fishing contests. As Visitor Services Director Tom Kellers told a *New York Times*

reporter, "There's no excuse for anyone—regardless of age—to say 'I have nothing to do, there isn't anything for me.'"

Administrative support grew with expanded Visitor Services programming. In August of 1971, Nancy Borchert, who grew up in Freehold and attended Freehold High School, came to work in the administrative office at Thompson Park. As she recalled, "we got notice that there was a job opening at the Park System. I graduated in June, had my interview, the Park System hired me, and I started in August." Over the years, Nancy has advanced thorough a number of positions to senior management in the Park System, and is the first female department head.

Park System staff opened historic Longstreet Farm in 1971 with farm machinery and livestock depicting the late 19th century era when agriculture was a way of life in the County. Naturalist Tom Kellers hired John Snyder to interpret the "farm scene," which included "2 horses, 2 ponies, 3 goats, 4 sheep, 3 pigs, 2 steer, 12 sheep, and 9 Bantam chickens for children to enjoy." "Farmer John," as Jim Truncer recalled, "had a personality that people enjoyed, and they came back as regulars because they loved talking with him."

NANCY BORCHERT, Senior Personnel Assistant

I love coming to work every day

When I started, we did a little bit of everything and worked for everybody. We took steno, worked the switchboard, took reservations. We had electric typewriters and we used carbon paper, so if you made a mistake, you had to correct every carbon. But there was opportunity for growth, and over time I came to really like the Park System and to believe in what it stands for.

In '85 I decided that I wanted to further my education. The Park System had the tuition reimbursement program, so I starting going to Brookdale Community College part-time at night for about six years... After I graduated, I went to Monmouth University and received my degree in business administration and management. Then I moved to Personnel. I've always liked working with people, working with the public, doing programs. I've liked the jobs and the employees, too. Every day they come in and say hello, and they're happy.

The employees know they have a beautiful place to work, and they appreciate that. I think it takes a certain kind of person to work in the parks, and they are the people who enjoy the outdoors and nature. It's hard to sit at a computer all day, but to be able to look up, look out the window, see the beautiful scenery... I love coming to work every day.

DOUG KRAMPERT, Chief Park Naturalist

Because we fished as kids, because we camped, I like the outdoors

Born and raised in Bergen County, Doug developed a love for the outdoors from family activities:

At a very young age, my brothers and I fished and camped together, in the backyard but also up in Bear Mountain in southern New York because that was fairly close to us. When we took family vacations, we did outdoor things and went into State parks and stayed in cabins there. So, from an early age I thought that I didn't want to work in an office. I wanted to get outdoors for my job.

I went to Utah State University where I could major in forestry and wildlife, and I graduated with a BS in fish biology in 1970. A game warden out there told me that his job not only involved science, but also talking with people and educating people, and I thought that would be kind of nice. I knew I liked dealing with people but didn't know I would like it as much as I do.

After a year and a half of working with Farmer John, I became full-time in June of '73 and started working with more of the naturalists. We did free nature walks, mostly in Turkey Swamp, Shark River, and Holmdel, and I had to learn about the natural environment on each one of the trails.

When you do a live snake show and the kids' faces light up, you see that you're kind of turning them on or you're teaching them. Sometimes kids are petrified of snakes and you get them to touch a snake and actually feel that a snake isn't slimy. It's great dealing with the kids because they keep you young.

Tom also hired Doug Krampert, who had recently graduated from Utah State University with a degree in biology, to help Farmer John. As Doug recalled, "We took school groups through the farm environment and we talked about the barns and about the hand-hewn logs that they were seeing, about some of the animals there. We talked about

When Longstreet Farm first opened, naturalists gave tours rather than costumed interpreters. Howard Wikoff, shown here in 1974, became Park Manager of Longstreet Farm, overseeing development of the living history programs, historical collections, and building restorations.

the equipment and how they used it at the turn of the century." That first year 13,000 children and adults visited Longstreet to see how corn was shelled, fields were plowed, and sheep were sheared. For many of those visitors it was their first time on a farm.

Part of our County's heritage

Park System staff started working in 1971 to preserve two very special properties in Upper Freehold Township. Jim Truncer knew the county significance of both properties and was determined to preserve them.

The 169-acre Clayton Farm, the first property, included 88 acres of mature forest along Doctor's Creek with majestic stands of oak and beech trees that exemplified the "Open Space Plan" criteria for a priority preservation site. Paul Clayton, then 88, had lived on the farm since he bought it in 1906. His daughter Thelma, then in her 60s, had lived there since her birth. As the Park System's appraisal noted, "The Claytons occupy the 200-year old dwelling under very primitive conditions. There is no indoor plumbing or gas, and the only water supply is from a dug well outside the back door which is equipped with a hand-operated pitcher pump."

The Claytons were regularly solicited by developers who wanted to subdivide their land and by lumbermen who wanted to harvest the

timber, but the Claytons wanted to see their farm preserved. Their friend Bob Zion, a nationally-known landscape architect who lived in nearby Imlaystown, championed the idea of preserving it as a County park, but acquiring land in the County's rural western corner was a tough sell at that time. Worried that the Claytons might not be able to wait until acquisition funds became available, Jim Truncer negotiated an option agreement with the Claytons that would enable the County to buy their farm below market value when it obtained funding, while allowing them to live there for the rest of Paul's life.

The 36-acre Walnford, the second property, is in the Crosswicks Creek stream valley, which the "Open Space Plan" had identified as a priority preservation area. Jim Truncer knew Walnford was one of the County's most important historic sites, with a 1772 Georgian house and a rare 1873 grist mill with intact machinery. In 1971, Jim wrote to William Meirs, whose family had owned Walnford for 200 years, to ask if he "might consider preserving it as a part of our county's heritage."

William Meirs was the great-great-great-grandson of Richard Waln, a Philadelphia Quaker who had built the house and whose granddaughter, Sarah Waln Hendrickson, had built the grist mill after a fire destroyed its predecessor. Meirs had never lived at Walnford but had maintained it. After vandals had burned down two historic houses on the property in 1969, Meirs had started to think seriously about selling it. He discussed the County's interest with Jim but ran out of patience while Park System staff tried to line up funding to buy it. As Meirs told a reporter, "The County hasn't made an offer. I've waited too long now… If someone comes to me with an agreement that is satisfactory, I'm not going to wait any longer."

Meirs contracted to sell Walnford to Ed and Joanne Mullen, who lived nearby on Fair Winds Farm, and he wrote to Jim Truncer, "I regret that you and the Park System had not been in a position to enter into an Agreement of Sale prior to this, as I would have liked to see it get into your hands."

Dave Moore, Director of the N.J. Conservation Foundation, offered to buy Walnford for the County and hold it until Green Acres funding came through, stating, "As far as we are concerned, Walnford is one of the most important acquisitions facing any county government in New Jersey today." When Jim told the Mullens that the County was intent on preserving Walnford by acquiring it for the Park System, they assured him that they "were not going to be doing something foolish with this place."

Ed Mullen wrote to Jim, "I want to confirm to you our intention to not only maintain and protect the Walnford property but hopefully improve it so that its value as an historic farm in Upper freehold Township will not be lost. We would also be willing to open the house occasionally for those groups who might find a particular interest in seeing it. With regard to the mill, I would hope to make it operative and as you suggested in some joint effort, make it possible for children's groups particularly to visit it…I hope that the Board will decide that this particular property will be well off in my hands." The Mullens acquired Walnford in 1973.

Irreplaceable public value

With its commanding view of Sandy Hook and New York City and its unique geology, Park System staff identified Mount Mitchill in Highlands and Atlantic Highlands as "a natural site for a county park." At an elevation of 266 feet, Mount Mitchill is the highest point on the Atlantic coast below southern Maine, and it has been a popular scenic overlook from the time Native Americans occupied the region. When a developer revealed plans in 1971 for two high rise towers on the 12–acre site, many people urged County leaders to preserve it.

The Park System designated Mount Mitchill as a high priority acquisition because of its "irreplaceable public value," and received Green Acres and U.S. Department of Housing and Urban Development (HUD) matching grants in 1972 to purchase 10.5 acres. Because the developer had rushed to start building one of the towers, the Freeholders had to settle for 7.1 acres. The *Asbury Park Press* reported, "Mount Mitchill Compromise Leaving Many Unsatisfied," as the outcome illustrated government's inability to compete against developers when timing was crucial. Assistance from land banks like the N.J. Conservation Foundation could help level the playing field in many, but not all, cases.

Green Acres and HUD also awarded matching grants to the Park System to finally preserve 476 acres of Hartshorne Woods, which Walter Schoellner had first targeted for preservation in 1965. Members of the Hartshorne Woods Association had also championed the preservation of the land for many years. When the Park System announced the acquisition of Hartshorne Woods, the *Asbury Park Press* lauded the preservation of this "prime public asset" for future generations.

The creation of Hartshorne Woods Park in 1973 proved timely because just a few months later the U.S. General Services Administration declared almost two-thirds of the adjacent 224-acre former Army H.A.A.D.S. facility as surplus property. Park System staff quickly applied to transfer the 161 undeveloped surplus acres to the County under President Nixon's "Legacy of Parks" program. The Federal Bureau of Outdoor Recreation completed the transfer to the County in the spring of 1974, and the Park System added it to Hartshorne Woods Park. The Bureau also transferred a 5-acre parcel known as the Middletown Radio Propagation Site to the County, and the Park System added it to Tatum Park. Competition for the 63-acre H.A.A.D. S. facility, which was now surrounded by Hartshorne Woods Park, and the Army's cleanup of the site would tie it up for many years, but County officials remained determined to add it to the Park.

The Recreation Commissioners opened their first golf course, Howell Park Golf Course, in 1972 to immediate acclaim from serious golfers. By the end of the season, more than 18,500 golfers had played at Howell Park, and many took lessons from the professional staff. To top off the accomplishment of building a first-rate golf course, the Park System received a HUD grant for a little more than half of the property's purchase price. When combined with the Green Acres funds already received, the acquisition cost to Monmouth taxpayers was, as Freeholder Theodore Narozanick wrote in a letter, "None."

Howell Park Golf Course, 1978.

Shark River Golf Course, 1970s.

With the growing interest in golf, County officials had also applied for Green Acres funding to preserve the 180-acre Asbury Park Golf and Country Club in Neptune Township, adjacent to Shark River Park. The City of Asbury Park, which owned the Club, could not wait for the County to line up funding and sold it to a developer that wanted to build 2,019 retirement homes on it. The Park System's appraisal noted that one-third of the site was undeveloped, with wooded lowlands and meadows fronting two and a half miles of the Shark River and Jumping Brook. Because the proposed intensive development would threaten these wetlands and stream corridors and destroy a valuable recreation facility, Neptune Township officials urged the County to acquire the Club to preserve its resources.

When the Park System finally received a Green Acres matching grant for the Club in 1973, the developer had already filed plans for its project. Noting that waiting times at Howell Park Golf Course could run up to two and a half hours, the Freeholders tried to negotiate a purchase from the developer, but ultimately had to preserve the Asbury Park Golf and Country Club through eminent domain. The Recreation Commissioners renamed the 18-hole facility the Shark River Golf Course.

In the summer of 1973, a generous gift of land and timely action created a big new park. Genevieve Hubbard Tatum told Recreation Commissioner Victor Grossinger that she was considering donating 73 acres of her 170-acre Indian Springs Farm in Middletown, where he had grown up and where his father had been farm manager.

Mrs. Tatum's father-in-law, Charles Tatum, had co-founded the Whitall Tatum Company, the oldest glass manufacturer in the United States, with factories in Keyport in northern Monmouth County and in Millville in Cumberland County. Charles Tatum bought the farm in 1905 as a summer home and named it Indian Springs after a natural spring on the site used by Native Americans, according to local lore. The property included an 18th century house built by Reverend William Bennett, a pastor of the Middletown and Holmdel Baptist Churches.

When Jim Truncer and Victor Grossinger asked Mrs. Tatum if the Park System could buy the rest of Indian Springs, she agreed, but they did not have the money because there was no Green Acres funding available. Jim showed the farm to Doug Hoff, the head of the Bureau of Outdoor Recreation in the U.S. Department of the Interior, who was impressed with both the land and Mrs. Tatum's donation. The Bureau subsequently awarded a grant from its Land and Water Conservation Fund to the County to buy the 97-acre portion, using Mrs. Tatum's 73-acre donation as a match. The Park System opened Tatum Park for nature programs in 1974.

In its natural state

The Park System's increasing success led to another generous donation that created a new park in 1974. Michael Huber of the Locust section of Middletown oversaw the Huber family's donation of 120 acres of mature forest along Brown's Dock Road. Mike's grandfather, Joseph M. Huber had bought the original 30 acres of the family farm in 1915 through his J.M. Huber Corporation. Mike's parents, Hans and Catherine Huber, built an Alpine-style house on the hill off Brown's Dock Road for their large family. Having enjoyed the farm for decades, the Hubers wanted to preserve the woods as "a nature sanctuary." They donated the land to the County "for park and conservation purposes and for no other purpose whatsoever," and requested that Brown's Dock Road be maintained in perpetuity as a "dirt road."

After the donation Mike wrote to Jim Truncer, "We are pleased to be able to have this tract preserved for the public to enjoy in its natural state. We are, in addition, thankful that there is a dedicated person like you to administer the County Park System, who also has the breadth of vision to plan an expanding park system to meet the future needs of the County, and who also sees the desirability of including in the Park System many different land uses, including a conservation area such as this one." Park naturalists soon started conducting nature walks through the dense forest of oaks, beeches, and tulip trees.

Left: Mike Huber at Huber Woods Park, 2006.

Below: Early 20th century postcard of Indian Springs Farm, now Tatum Park.

Indian Spring Farm, Country Residence of C. A. Tatum, Middletown, N. J.

In June of 1974, Holmdel native John Hoffman came to work for the Park System full time after graduating from college. John had worked the previous summer at Turkey Swamp Park, and as he recalled, "I interviewed with Bruce Gollnick and then sat down with Jim Truncer and he offered me the job, so I was very pleased and fortunate to have a job two miles from my home. Jim's a strong believer in hiring people right out of college. He likes to get them young, and then he tends to mold and set their direction." John retired as Superintendent of Recreation in 2009 after 35 years with the Park System.

Park System staff noted in their 1974 Annual Report that "Howell Park Golf Course hosted over 43,000 golfers and is an example of a recreation bargain of major proportions. For those who do not play golf, the open fields, green spaces, and clean air are an added bonus." The Park System earned 22% of its operating budget from greens fees at Howell Park and Shark River Golf Courses and from activity fees at Turkey Swamp and Thompson Parks. In developing the Park System's Trust Fund from revenues, Jim Truncer recalled, "We first sold soda from vending machines loaned to us and used the money to buy new boats and canoes, and then expanded the fund from several hundred dollars to what it is today—about $10.1 million."

A very desirable property

Voters approved the third Green Acres Bond Act in November, 1974, for $200 million, and in early 1975, an extraordinary opportunity arose for the Park System to build on its accomplishments at the Howell Park and Shark River Golf Courses. The Mercer family of Rumson offered to sell Hominy Hill, their private golf course in Colts Neck, to the Park System.

Henry Mercer created the golf course in 1965 and had recently retired as Chairman of States Marine Corporation, an international shipping company he founded in 1931. Mercer bought Hominy Hill Farm in 1941 to raise Guernsey and Charolais cattle and gradually increased the farm to over 400 acres. An enthusiastic yachtsman and owner of the racing sloop "Weatherly" that won the America's Cup in 1962, Mercer enjoyed golfing and entertaining his many business associates and friends. In 1963, he commissioned the prominent golf course architect Robert Trent Jones of Montclair to design an 18-hole course on 180 acres of his farm.

As Jim Truncer recalled, "They adapted the barn into the clubhouse and the calf barn became the pro shop. He created Hominy Hill for his guests and had a pro there. He made the golf course available on

JOHN HOFFMAN
Superintendent of
Recreation, 1985–2009

*It's been a great place
to work*

A lifelong resident of Holmdel, John Hoffman recalled visiting Holmdel Park as a child. "I would walk to the sledding hill from Holmdel Village, probably a mile and a half. There were still a lot of farms in Holmdel at the time." John worked as a lifeguard at the ocean while he was in high school and later graduated from East Carolina University in Greenville, North Carolina. As he recalled,

I went there as a liberal arts major. After freshman year, I heard about the parks and recreation program and decided it was really in line with what I enjoyed doing in my leisure time—outdoor recreation like whitewater canoeing, kayaking, rafting, sailing—so it seemed to be a perfect match. The program had a variety of courses, from conservation, geology, basic biology, to outdoor recreation programs. My area was recreation administration.

The summer prior to graduating from college, I worked at Turkey Swamp where I was in charge of the paddleboats, rowboats, and canoes. Before that, I was a volunteer leader for the outdoor recreation department for a couple of years, under Alan Jennings, the original outdoor recreation supervisor.

I started working full time in June, 1974 in the park operations office to get an orientation to the park system. Then they gave me a couple of parks to oversee, Hartshorne Woods and Huber. After that I moved over to the land acquisition department, and then I moved to recreation as assistant superintendent, and in 1985 I became Superintendent of Recreation.

The long view is, it has been a great place to work and we've been very fortunate. I think most people here are in the positions they're in because they have a passion for it. So we're very lucky. We have some great people. Our environmental educators, our outdoor recreation people, our therapeutic staff, they all just do a great job.

Hominy Hill Golf Course, 1983.

some Fridays to local charities, but it was mainly invited guests who got to play there. It was not heavily used at all. If you drove by and saw a saw a foursome, you would think it was a busy day at Hominy Hill."

The Park System's appraisal of Hominy Hill noted, "This excellent 18-hole championship golf course designed by Jones has been lavishly cared for and appears to be a very desirable property." Jim Truncer recalled that when he showed the appraised value to Dick Mercer, Henry Mercer's son, "Dick said, 'That's right in the ballpark of what we thought it would be.' I said, 'Well, I'll need time to line up Green Acres funding, and also to get the Freeholders on board,' and he agreed to that."

Local opposition delayed the purchase and a group of would-be buyers sued to block it. Some citizens also doubted the Park System's ability to maintain such a fine golf course for the general public. During the 18 months that it took to secure the funding and approvals, Dick Mercer never wavered from his verbal agreement. As Jim remembered, "The harder people tried to undo this, the firmer Dick's handshake. In fact, the Mercers maintained the golf course and replaced equipment just as though they were going to own it forever. That's the kind of people the Mercers are."

Hundreds of eager golfers played their first rounds at Hominy Hill

Monmouth County Fair,
East Freehold Park, 1982.

DAVE COMPTON
Superintendent of Parks

*Maintaining and providing
those places that I grew up
enjoying*

Dave was born in the farming region of southern Illinois
and moved with his family to
Michigan at the age of six, as he
recalled:

*Both my grandparents
owned farms in Illinois, and
from about eight years old, the
day after I got out of school I was on a bus that ran from Jackson,
Michigan to Mt. Carmel, Illinois. I would spend summers with my
grandparents working on their farms...feeding the animals, helping in the fields, baling hay, plus a little fishing and playing.*

*When I went to Michigan State, it had a natural resource
division, with a park and recreation resources department that
emphasized interpretation, resource management, and planning. I
entered the program because it just seemed to fit with my interest
of being outdoors and spending a lot of time in parks. I had done
a lot of camping and backpacking while growing up, so it just
seemed to fit with maintaining and providing those places that I
grew up enjoying.*

*The Park System is a great place to work, a lot of good people, a
lot of opportunities. I enjoy coming to work every day.*

when the Park System opened it in 1977. The *Red Bank Register* reported, "Golfers called the course 'superb,' while county officials breathed
a sigh of relief. 'This has been a long, hard struggle,' said Freeholder
Director Harry Larrison, who stood firmly behind the purchase when
it was attacked in the courts. 'We have preserved something for our
children and our children's children.'" After all the controversy, Hominy
Hill would prove to be one of the Park System's finest facilities and one
of the top public golf courses in the country.

By the end of its first season in 1977, Hominy Hill Golf Course had become the Park System's biggest source of revenue, earning 50% more
than the golf course at Howell Park. The three golf courses together
earned 74% of total Park System revenues, and these revenues equaled
36% of the Park System's operating costs.

The Park System developed a major partnership in 1975 when the
Monmouth County 4-H Association was looking for a new site to
hold its annual 4-H Fair. Tom Kellers initiated an agreement with 4-H
to co-sponsor a fair at East Freehold Park, which the Park System had
acquired in 1970. Over the July 4th weekend, the first joint fair attracted
9,000 people with programs, displays, and competitions, and this collaboration between 4-H and the Park System has continued ever since.
Tom supervised the Monmouth County/4-H Fair for the first two years
and then passed it on to another Park System staff person, Bob Cain.
Since then, rotating the position of County Fair Chairman among staff
has become a Park System tradition.

In the fall of 1975 Jim Truncer hired Dave Compton as the first
County Park Manager. After graduating that June from Michigan State
University where he studied Park and Recreation Administration, Dave
was recommended to Jim by Roger Murray, a Michigan State profes-

sor who had worked at the Park System as the first Superintendent
of Parks. After completing his initial assignment, Dave assumed the
management of Holmdel Park. He became Assistant Superintendent of
Parks in 1981 and has served as Superintendent of Parks since 1985.

In the spring of 1976 Marjorie Wihtol of Middletown contacted Jim
Truncer to discuss Deep Cut Farm, her 39-acre property on Red Hill
Road opposite Tatum Park. The 39-acre site had an unusual history and
contained remnants of elaborate gardens installed by reputed mobster
Vito Genovese when he had owned the property between 1935 and
1948. Mrs. Wihtol and her husband Karl had purchased the farm in 1952
and built a house on the high bluff along Red Hill Road.

As Jim Truncer recalled, "Mrs. Wihtol was well-educated, had gone
to the Sorbonne, had traveled the world, and was interested in a lot of

Deep Cut Farm in 1954, when it was owned by Karl and Marjorie Wihtol. On the opposite side of the road are the former Middletown Radio Propagation Site and Indian Hill Farm, both now part of Tatum Park.

things. She had previously called, wondering if we were interested in some of the plants on the property. She wasn't prepared to donate the property outright. She had a son, and she wanted to provide for him as well. She agreed to leave half to the County upon her death and to give us six months to purchase the other half." When she died in 1977, Mrs. Wihtol bequeathed half the farm for "park and horticultural purposes only…and it shall be known as Deep Cut Park." Park System staff secured a Green Acres matching grant to buy the other half of the farm from her estate and opened Deep Cut Gardens in 1978.

One of the last sizable, undeveloped tracts east of Highway 35

The 1970 "Open Space Plan" had identified the 113-acre Weltz Farm on the Ocean Township-Eatontown border as one of five "Proposed County Park Sites." Calling the site "one of the last sizable, undeveloped tracts east of Highway 35," Joseph Palaia, Mayor of Ocean Township, wrote to Jim in 1976 that, "The Weltz tract is particularly desirable as a park site. It is rolling, well-drained, picturesque, and easily accessible. The farm was active as a dairy farm until a few years ago and maintains a pastoral calm. Mr. Weltz's pond and an unusually handsome stand of Buttonwood trees along the road remain today. The Township heartily supports the 'Open Space Plan' for the development of a County Park in the highly-populated areas east of Highway 35 and we urge the purchase of the Weltz Farm while this desirable land remains intact."

Although Park System officials lacked funding to acquire the Weltz Farm, they did not want to lose it to development. They arranged with Dave Moore, the Director of the N.J. Conservation Foundation, to have the Foundation purchase and hold the property until the Park System secured a Green Acres matching grant. Mayor Palaia told an *Asbury Park Press* reporter that he was "very, very happy with the proposed sale…We owe a great indebtedness to Mr. Weltz, who has taken a liking to our town and thinks about its welfare. He could have sold that tract for a lot more money to a developer to build on. He likes to look at the open spaces the same as we do." When a developer proposed subdividing the adjacent 29-acre parcel into "Lenape Estates," the Foundation also bought and held it for the Park System.

The N.J. Conservation Foundation soon helped the Park System preserve two more key parcels of open space. In the fall of 1976, Bruce Huber from the Riverside Drive Association in Locust wrote to Jim Truncer about the 52-acre Drazin property on Brown's Dock Road that developers were eyeing, "In our opinion it would be in the best

interests in our locality and the county at large, if this property could be purchased by the county to join the two Huber parks to provide a continuous park. This property, if left in its natural state, will provide for this generation and future generations a parkland of unsurpassed beauty. No comparable natural acreage exists in Monmouth County." The 148-acre Deepdale tract, "a vital ecological area" next to Tatum Park in Middletown, was also being eyed by developers.

The Foundation bought both of these parcels at the Park System's request, and was now holding four properties until the Park System could secure Green Acres grants to preserve them. The *Red Bank Register* praised the Foundation in December, 1976 for "performing a valuable public service." The cooperation between the Foundation and the Park System, the *Register* noted, "not only saves the more valuable open lands from development for lesser uses, but also protects the taxpayers from possible spiraling land prices."

When a Middletown official interested in tax ratables complained about "losing property to the county so that it could be left in its natural state," the *Register* commented, "It would be shortsighted to look upon open-space areas as 'lost' or wasted. The ecological and aesthetic values of such lands are inestimable to a neighborhood and a community, as much an asset to property values as good schools and good municipal services. Middletown is fortunate that the County Park System has permitted it to retain those values."

Faster than the County government

By mid-1977, the N.J. Conservation Foundation was anxious for the County to purchase the four properties it was holding for the Park System so that it could free up its resources for land preservation projects in other counties. Jim asked Mike Huber for his help with this situation, as Mike recalled, "I got involved early on when Jim felt that it would be worthwhile to have a non-profit land trust in the area which could move faster than the County government at times. He had been working with the N.J. Conservation Foundation, but they felt they spent too much of their effort in this area because Jim had a lot going on and used them quite a bit. They were very happy to help us get started and set up the Monmouth Conservation Foundation. I remember being in very early conversations with Jim Truncer and Dave Moore and various other people, including Chet Apy and Larry Carton. We met at Hominy Hill, upstairs. Chet subsequently devoted a lot of time and effort to the acquisition of land for the Foundation and the Park System."

"Our Monmouth Conservation Foundation"
Green Heritage, June – July 1980

The ability of a foundation to move quickly to acquire lands needed for future open space in parks assures the public that the land is protected and available until the town or county is in a position to move forward. Often, a municipality is unable to act in time on its own, due to the time periods required to raise money and get state and federal financial aid approved. Fortunately for those of us who live in Monmouth County, the Monmouth Conservation Foundation may be able to save some of our last remaining open space before land is lost to development or other uses. The Foundation is particularly interested in working to save farmland and to encourage agriculture to stay in Monmouth County.

Since its founding in 1977, and under the leadership of its long-time President Judith Stanley Coleman, the Monmouth Conservation Foundation has helped preserve over 6,000 acres at 42 sites, including 1,861 acres for the Park System, County farmland preservation projects, and many municipal projects as well.

Chester Apy, an attorney who grew up in Little Silver and served on the Borough Council, in the State Assembly, and as an administrative law judge, remembered when Jim approached him about starting a foundation, "Jim knew the people around the County and he put together the original invitation list when we had our first gathering out at Hominy Hill Golf Course. He got Dave Moore to speak and people signed up that night to be involved, and that group became the original Board of Directors of the Monmouth Conservation Foundation. Judy and Bob Stanley were in that original group, Natalie Beglin, and George Illmensee who was a real estate broker and a farm owner in Colts Neck, and Mike Slovak, the President of Steinbach's department store in Asbury Park and in Red Bank. He was the original president of the Foundation."

Both the N.J. Conservation Foundation and the Monmouth Conservation Foundation would soon help the Park System preserve a very important property.

The smiles on their faces in the pictures really show it

The Visitor Services staff of the Park System launched a number of new programs in 1976 and 1977. They started the "Volunteers in Parks" program, as *Green Heritage* reported in November-December 1976, to "provide unique opportunities for all people in our county...to learn from the Park System's Professional Staff, and to assist them in conducting a variety of activities. Volunteers will attend orientation and training sessions to become fully acquainted with the skills and philosophies involved before reporting to their chosen fields. Currently, volunteers are needed in Land Management, Fine Arts, Outdoor Recreation, Nature Activities, Gardening, and Tournaments. The only requirements for participants is that they be energetic, enthusiastic, and above the age of 13."

Park naturalists opened the Holmdel Park Activity Center on Longstreet Road in the spring of 1977 with offices, displays, and activity rooms, and from there they led nature walks around the park. The Activity Center represented a major turning point, as Doug Krampert

Park System naturalists about 1977, from left: Patty O'Rourke, Gerry Savitz, Doug Krampert, Andrew Coeyman and Robert Henschel.

Left: Building a Lenni Lenape Longhouse, a favorite program for school groups, in 1981.

Right: Park System Ranger Bruce Egeland in 1968, wearing an early ranger uniform.

recalled, "Nick Fiorillo and I had philosophical discussions as to whether we should start charging for programs. We would often have a group schedule a nature walk at Holmdel Park, and they wouldn't show. So the feeling was, if we start charging people something, they're going to think that this program is worth something. We started charging for day-long school programs, and we did a lot with fourth grades as a unit of studies on the Lenni Lenape Indians, the Native Americans in New Jersey. We were also starting to realize that if we wanted to do more things, we needed a way of generating income and getting away from a strictly operating budget. I feel over the years that this has really helped the Park System."

As the demand for nature programs kept growing, Visitor Services staff launched a series of Group Discovery Activities in 1979 from the Holmdel Park Activity Center. As Doug Krampert recalled, "We decided to do more day-long programs. Nick Fiorillo developed the Longhouse program. Bob Henschel and I came up with a birdhouse building program, where we did a slide program on the native birds and then the kids went out and actually built a bird house. We developed the fossil program where we went down into the Shark River with one to two groups of kids, maybe fifty or sixty kids. We built a fossil screen about a foot square and they used that to dig up fossil shark teeth in the river. We all worked together as a staff and perfected the programs."

Following one of these sessions, Keyport teacher Bruce Davidson wrote to Nick Fiorillo, "The students found the experience interesting, valuable, and enjoyable. For some of them it was the first time they caught a fish or even had a rod and reel in their hands. The Longhouse

gave the students a real sense of accomplishment and the smiles on their faces in the pictures really show it."

After three 7th-grade programs, Barbara McEvoy, Vocations Coordinator of Plumsted Township, wrote to the Recreation Commissioners, "These trips were excellent educational experiences for our students. They not only learned a great deal, but also enjoyed the trips tremendously. The success of these trips was largely due to Mr. Fiorillo's excellent talent as a teacher and his very fine rapport with our students. He made the study fascinating and the experience great fun. Thank you for providing a unique and invaluable educational experience for our students."

With the increasing number of visitors and parks, the Park System developed a training program to help Park Rangers develop, as *Green Heritage* reported in November-December 1977, "the skills necessary to perform their unique, dual roles as stewards of both the visiting public and the natural resources of the parks." The "dual role" of rangers involves protecting visitors and helping them enjoy the parks, while also maintaining facilities to protect the County's investment and to provide positive experiences for visitors. In 200 hours of training, Park System staff and professionals from other organizations orient rangers to the variety of facilities and services in the Park System and help them develop communication and maintenance skills.

The outcome was worth waiting for

The Park System was finally able to acquire the four properties that the N.J. Conservation Foundation was holding for it in 1979. After State voters had approved the fourth Green Acres Bond Act in 1978 for $200 million, the Park System secured Green Acres matching grants to buy the Weltz Farm and another parcel to create Weltz Park, to add the Deepdale Tract to Tatum Park, and to add the Drazin parcel to Huber Woods Park. With these acquisitions at the end of the decade, there were now 19 parks preserving nearly 4,200 acres. The Park System secured another Green Acres matching grant that year to finally preserve the Clayton Farm in Upper Freehold Township. As the *Asbury Park Press* reported on May 25, 1979,

The purchase by the County climaxed five years of waiting by 94-year-old Paul Clayton, who bought the farm in 1906, and his daughter, Thelma, who has lived there all her life. The Claytons are elated that the fields and woods they love so well have been saved from the developers. For years, said Ms. Clayton, they have been

Paul Clayton and Thelma Clayton in the 1990s.

'pestered' to sell off lots, and lumbermen 'tortured us to death' for permission to cut the trees. One in particular vowed he'd get the wood eventually, 'but we've both outlived him.' Sitting around the dining room table last week, the Claytons got the news of the Green Acres approval from Spencer H. Wickham, chief of acquisition and design for the park system, and he apologized for the long delay since the first option was taken five years ago. Miss Clayton said the outcome was worth waiting for and she praised the pleasant manner in which Wickham and Truncer handled the negotiations. 'They were always gentlemen,' she said.

A priceless gift

After living at Walnford for six years with their five children, Joanne and Ed Mullen decided to donate the historic site on Crosswicks Creek in Upper Freehold to the Park System. Their generous donation included the 1772 Georgian house, the intact 1873 grist mill, multiple farm buildings, historic furnishings and equipment, and 36 acres. As Joanne told a Newark *Star Ledger* reporter, "My husband and I wanted to be sure Walnford would be preserved properly." The Mullens had taken excellent care of the property, replacing roofs, upgrading utilities, and making structural repairs. "It was like having a treasure," Joanne said, "and we didn't want to do anything to lose the historical

value. I will be sad to leave, but it's important for a place like this to be preserved."

To enable the Park System to raise matching funds, the Mullens transferred the property at the end of 1979 to the N.J. Conservation Foundation, which transferred it in 1980 to the Monmouth Conservation Foundation to hold until the Park System could secure a Green Acres matching grant to acquire adjacent land along Crosswicks Creek. In a December 29, 1979 editorial on the donation, the *Red Bank Register* stated, "The Walnford tract is a welcome addition to the County's holdings of environmentally and historically irreplaceable lands, and all of us must be grateful to the Mullens for a priceless gift."

Walnford, 1992.

THE MULLENS' donation of Walnford demonstrated again that preservation of open space often involves preserving historic sites as well. In 1980, Joseph Hammond, Director of the Monmouth County Historical Association in Freehold, suggested to Jim Truncer that a countywide survey of historic sites would help government agencies and private owners understand the significance of the County's historic resources and their potential impact on open space preservation. They decided to collaborate on the project and, with a matching grant from the State Historic Preservation Office, the Park System hired two architectural historians, Gail Hunton and Jim McCabe, to conduct the survey. Through their Monmouth County Historic Sites Inventory they identified and documented nearly 2,000 historic properties, and this information has become increasingly valuable both as a planning resource for the County and its municipalities and as a record of the many historic buildings that have since been lost to development or abandonment.

Hard work made us believe in ourselves

The County's rich agricultural heritage includes an historic African American community along Red Hill Road in Middletown. To preserve some of that community's history and to honor her parents, Bertha Heath of Middletown was the guiding force behind her family's contribution to the Heath Wing, an expansion of the Tatum Park Activity Center that was dedicated in 1981 in honor of her parents Clinton P. and Mary E. Heath. As the youngest of thirteen children, Miss Heath fondly remembered her happy childhood growing up on her parents' farm, where "farm life and hard work made us believe in ourselves and our parents made us believe in ourselves."

Longstreet Farm in Holmdel Park epitomized the melding of open spaces and historic places. While the Park System staff had adapted historic buildings at Thompson and Tatum Parks for operational and recreational uses, their restoration of the Longstreet Farmhouse, completed in 1983, was the Park System's first authentic restoration to interpret a historic site. Howard Wikoff, the Senior Park Manager at Holmdel Park, guided the careful restoration to provide, as Jim Brown noted in the *Asbury Park Press*, "an intimate look into a farm home in the Victorian period." With the expanded 'living history' tour now including the house, Longstreet Farm became an even more popular destination for families and school groups who wanted to experience a glimpse of the County's agricultural past.

Opposite page: Clayton Park.

Cross Farm, preserved as open space by Holmdel Township. The documentation of this historic farmstead in the Monmouth County Historic Sites Inventory has assisted Holmdel's ongoing preservation efforts.

Bertha Heath (right) at the 1993 African American Celebration.

The Park System's expanded programming proved quite timely in 1980, as rising oil prices forced people to look for leisure time opportunities close to home. Visitor Services staff distributed 150,000 copies of its quarterly program calendar that summer and, thanks to an upgraded phone reservation system, enrolled over 300,000 County residents and visitors in programs representing "a myriad of activities for all to enjoy."

The staff offered programs and activities for residents of all ages and interests—from tots to seniors, from swimmers to sculptors. For lovers of the outdoors, Outdoor Recreation staff ran local and remote hiking trips to New York and Pennsylvania, summer camps (including the very

The Longstreet Farmhouse during restoration, 1981.

At Longstreet Farm, school children in the 1980s learn about how food was grown in the 1890s.

physical and mental disabilities, Therapeutic Recreation staff established programs in horseback riding, dancing, arts and crafts, camping, hiking, and sports.

With the Parks as their classrooms, Nature Interpretation staff conducted gardening programs, nature hikes, frog and fossil hunts, fishing and birding expeditions, Indian pottery and Longhouse programs, photo safaris, wildlife art shows, and canoe trips in the Pine Barrens. They also organized Shark River Park and Turkey Swamp Park Days with outdoor programs from 10 a.m. to 10 p.m., as well as trips to the Philadelphia Zoo and the National Museum of Natural History in Washington, DC.

The Park System received two significant boosts in 1981 in recognition of the quality of its golf facilities and management. Will Nicholson,

More than we could have hoped for

November 10, 1980
Mr. Nick Fiorillo
Monmouth County Park System

Dear Mr. Fiorillo,
Your new Pine Barrens program, from initial contact to pulling the last canoe out of the water, could not have been handled more professionally, sensitively, and enthusiastically than it was handled by Doug Krampert.
The Jonathon School is a private, nonprofit school for neurologically impaired and emotionally disturbed adolescent youngsters. The reason I chose this program was so that the students could face a new challenge, could find resources in themselves they weren't aware of, and could experience success at a difficult task. Our students are not easy to deal with. They have many problems ranging from physical to emotional.
Doug made our trip successful. His patience and sensitivity were essential to help these kids succeed. He was firm and clear about safety and encouraging and rewarding about their attempts. I feel we accomplished more than we could have hoped for. I look forward to more activities with the Monmouth County Park System. I hope Doug will be involved with all of them.

Sincerely, Lew Gantwerk,
Director, The Jonathon School, Marlboro, New Jersey

popular Outdoor Odyssey adventures), canoe clinics and races, whitewater rafting trips, and instructional workshops in sailing, bicycling, lifesaving, racquet sports, soccer, and belly dancing. Cultural Services' staff offered programs in fine and performing arts and handicrafts, as well as musical performances in the parks and trips to regional museums and New York City cultural events. For youngsters and adults with

Thompson Park Day, one of several family-oriented events initiated in the 1980s, offered games, music and crafts. First held in 1981 in the spring, Thompson Park Day is now a popular fall event.

President of the United States Golf Association (USGA), announced in the spring that it had selected Hominy Hill Golf Course as the site of the 58th United States Amateur Public Links Championship to be held in July, 1983. Only one other golf course in New Jersey had ever hosted this annual championship. Dave Pease, the Park System's General Manager of golf courses, called the USGA's selection of Hominy Hill "a validation of the conditioning and the other things we were able

The Park System commissioned local artist Donald Voorhees to illustrate a poster for the USGA's 58th Amateur Public Links Championship in 1983.

58th United States Golf Association Amateur Public Links Championship

**Hominy Hill Golf Course
Colts Neck, N.J.**

July 11-16, 1983

Special People United to Ride
Therapeutic Riding Program at Thompson Park
Green Link July-August 1981

The objective of therapeutic riding is to relieve the rider's disability as much is possible through a prescribed riding program. Disabled persons benefit in two ways: muscle strength, mobility, balance, coordination, and functions of the heart and lungs improve, and contracted muscles relax, improving the general physical condition of the rider. In addition, riders develop improved awareness, body image, and self-confidence.

Horseback riding has unique values for all. Relating with love to a large warm animal, socializing with a group of riders, and being responsible for providing basic care for the horse are beneficial experiences for anyone learning to ride. For those who are disabled, these take on even deeper meanings.

Left to right: Jerry Coburn on Rocky, SPUR president Carol Dorward, SPUR founder Mary Alice Goss, Kim Oswald on The Cisco Kid, Carl Twitchell, and Sally Vaun. 1981.

to achieve with the resources, the flexibility, and the commitment to produce a public facility of this quality."

Also in 1981, Hovnanian Enterprises, Inc. of Red Bank, one of the nation's largest homebuilders, donated its 64-acre Pine Brook Golf Course in Manalapan Township to the County. Hovnanian had built Pine Brook within its Covered Bridge adult community in the 1970s as an 18-hole "executive course," which is shorter in length than a regular golf course for golfers who want to play shorter games. Hovnanian officials told the Freeholders that they wanted to turn the golf course over to the

Ranger Graduation Ceremony, 2005;
Officer James Fay presents certificate
to Ranger Kelli McDonald.

County because it would do an "excellent job" of maintaining it. Pine Brook provided a new level of play for County golfers, and it was the only public golf course in the northwestern part of the County.

In the summer of 1981 the Park System began a collaboration that has brought enormous benefit and enjoyment to a special population of Monmouth County residents. Along with other riding enthusiasts, Mary Alice Goss, a Middletown horsewoman trained in therapeutic riding, created Special People United to Ride (SPUR) to help children and adults with disabilities develop skills and confidence through horseback riding. When the non-profit organization received four donated horses to start the program, Park System staff set up space for it in a stable at Thompson Park. Since that small beginning, the collaboration between the Park System and SPUR has achieved far more than any of its initiators could have dreamed.

In January, 1982, the Park System honored the first of its rangers to graduate from a new ranger training program at the Monmouth County Police Academy. This was the first program held in the State under the New Jersey Police Training Commission's new mandate for the training of all county park rangers. Designed to enhance cooperation between the rangers and local police departments, the program included much of the same training given to regular police officers in such procedures as interviews, arrests, evidence gathering, report writing, and crowd control. With this program, the Park System's rangers reached a new level of professionalism that kept them in the forefront of county park rangers in the State and across the country.

Of primary importance

To keep pace with the many changes going on around the County, Park System staff in 1983 completed the "Monmouth County Open

Space Guide," providing the first update to the land preservation goals identified in the County's 1970 "Open Space Plan." The 1983 "Open Space Guide" called for a natural resources inventory and a comprehensive mapping system for County and municipal agencies showing natural areas, existing open space and recreational areas, areas lacking open space, and proposed acquisitions. The Guide specified that the Park System should "periodically survey recreational needs and leisure activities and update the public about open space preservation needs and goals." It also noted that, "The preservation of historic sites in Monmouth County and in the Nation is essential. The history that is preserved will guide and educate the area into the future. Those historic sites which may be considered open space should be of primary importance in acquisition development and planning."

We are thrilled

In October, 1983, the Park System's nearly two-decade-long effort to obtain the U.S. Army's former Highlands Army Air Defense Site (H.A.A.D.S.), now surrounded by Hartshorne Woods Park, suffered

"Monmouth County Open Space Guide," 1983

Open space preservation, whether it be for forest conservation, farmland preservation, recreational development, stream valley preservation, or protection of historic sites, is and should continue to be a major emphasis in Monmouth County. Priorities for open space designation in Monmouth County are:

1. Unique environmental areas including wetlands, coastal beaches, aquifer recharge areas, stream corridors, floodplains, and areas supporting sensitive ecosystems.

2. Areas with significant natural and cultural resources such as historical or archaeological sites, wildlife habitats, woodlands, and farmlands.

3. Areas in an urban situation where open space and recreation deficits are apparent and population density great.

4. Areas which provide access to existing open space, recreation areas, or areas of high usability potential, including abandoned railroad rights-of-way and utility rights-of-way.

5. Areas which surround existing recreation or open space areas to act as an undeveloped buffer.

6. Areas easily accessible by major transportation routes.

another setback. The U.S. General Services Administration denied the Park System's request for a no-cost transfer of the site, in keeping with President Reagan's executive order to sell surplus property rather than transferring it at no cost to state or local governments.

Because of the County's long-standing interest in the site, the GSA subsequently offered to sell it to the County before offering it to the public for development. Park System Director Jim Truncer responded that the County did not have the funds to purchase the property and that its steep slopes would be unsuitable for any development other than recreation. Refusing to give up on a free transfer, County leaders turned to Congressman Jim Howard and Senator Bill Bradley for assistance. Thanks to their efforts, Interior Secretary James Watt announced a few months later that GSA would convey the site at no cost to the County. When a reporter asked Jim Truncer how County and Park System officials and staff felt after working so hard and long to preserve this key site, he replied, "We are thrilled." The GSA transfer of the 63-acre property in 1984 finally integrated the core of the former H.A.A.D.S. facility into Hartshorne Woods Park.

In November of 1983, New Jersey voters approved by a more than 2 to 1 margin the fifth Green Acres Bond Referendum for $135 million, including a new "Green Trust" low interest loan program, for open space acquisition and development. As Jim Truncer told a reporter, "This vote speaks well for how the public feels about parks, recreation, and open space preservation, and also for what has been accomplished since the first Green Acres Bond Issue in 1961. I cannot think of

anything since the Civilian Conservation Corps—the CCC—in the 1930s that has had as big an impact as the Green Acres program in providing public recreation opportunities for the citizens of our State."

With the assistance of grants from Green Acres and the Federal Land and Water Conservation Fund, the Park System began extensive redevelopment of Seven Presidents Oceanfront Park. After operating the beach site since 1977 under an agreement with the City of Long Branch, the Park System acquired it as the County's first oceanfront park early in 1984.

The initial redevelopment plan for the beachfront called for clean-up of the entire site, restoration of dunes, and the construction of a pavilion with outdoor showers, parking, and a maintenance area. The City had previously used an old house near the beach as a lifeguard station, but it was slated for demolition because vandals had badly damaged it. The Monmouth County Historic Sites Inventory had identified the house as the "Navaho Lodge," the sole survivor of nine shingled cottages in "The Reservation," an exclusive enclave built around 1900 by Nate Salsbury, the principal owner of William F. "Buffalo Bill" Cody's Wild West Show. Considering the history of the house and local sentiment to preserve it, Park System officials decided to move it to the northwest end of the park and renovate it for an Activity Center and park offices. Today, "Navaho Lodge" provides a glimpse of the turn-of-the-century era when seven U.S. Presidents summered in Long Branch.

Navaho Lodge at Seven Presidents Park in Long Branch during its 1983 move.

The Highlands Army Air Defense Site (H.A.A.D.S.), which housed the Missile Master control facility for the Nike missile defense of New York, seen here in the 1980s prior to demolition by the U.S. Army Corps of Engineers.

Marlu Farm and Cheeca Farm, looking northeast over the Swimming Reservoir, 1985.

Threatening the very resources that make the watersheds so important

Since the creation of its "Recreation Study and Plan" in 1960, the County had advocated the preservation of land along Swimming River to protect the water supply in the populous northeastern part of the County. Following up on the watershed protection reiterated in the 1983 "Open Space Guide," Park System staff identified two high-priority sites on the Swimming River Reservoir for acquisition with Green Acres funding in the 1980s: the contiguous Cheeca Farm and Marlu Farm straddling Holmdel and Middletown Townships. The two scenic historic farm properties comprised nearly 450 acres of prime farmland from the west boundary of Thompson Park to Longbridge Road, and from Newman Springs Road to the Swimming River Reservoir. Marlu Farm had once been part of Brookdale Farm, now Thompson Park, and Cheeca Farm formed a hilly peninsula extending into Swimming River Reservoir. Park

System staff appraised the properties, amicably discussed the County's interest with the owners, obtained the endorsement of the Middletown and Holmdel mayors, and submitted Green Acres applications.

County and Park System officials were stunned by news in April 1984 that both property owners had contracted to sell their farms to developers for cash. Like similar situations noted earlier, the property owners were unwilling to wait for Green Acres funding and County approvals. The Freeholders, Recreation Commissioners, and Park System staff were all determined to preserve the farms to protect the Swimming River watershed and to buffer Thompson Park from the impact of development, but their quest was now a lot harder and would be considerably more expensive.

The developers convinced Holmdel officials to change the zoning for the properties from single family homes to townhouses and presented plans to build 454 houses, a Holmdel Golf and Country Club with a 25-acre lake, and a 160,000 gallon per day septic treatment plant. When the developers stated that their project would have little effect on traffic, a Middletown official predicted that it would "choke" Newman Springs Road.

In a study titled "Land Use in the Swimming River and Manasquan River Reservoir Watersheds," the County Planning Board characterized the development situation in the watersheds as "urgent and pressing" and recommended prohibiting the extension of sanitary sewer service in the watersheds and the preservation of "critical and unique" tracts. The study noted that, "All of the resources the watersheds provide are part of what makes Monmouth County a desirable place to live… unfortunately, much of the development occurring in the watersheds is threatening the very resources that make the watersheds so important…These watersheds provide the County with a diversity of natural and cultural resources. The Swimming River Reservoir is a source of potable surface water for nearly one half of the County's population."

The Freeholders continued trying to purchase the two farms but lost their patience when the developers demolished the historic Peter Smock House, an important Greek Revival dwelling on Marlu Farm, without a permit. The developer's rash actions and the solid support of Middletown officials and area residents, hundreds of whom came out to a public meeting to voice their opposition to the development and their support for preserving the properties, made the politically difficult decision easier for the Freeholders. In May, 1985, they unanimously approved the acquisition of both farms by eminent domain to protect the Swimming River watershed and Thompson Park. The various approvals that the developers had received from Holmdel Township for their plans more than quadrupled the acquisition cost.

One month later, the Freeholders announced another key acquisition on the Swimming River Reservoir for the Park System, the 381-acre Dorbrook Farm in Colts Neck Township. Murray M. Rosenberg, the former majority owner of the Miles Shoes Company of New York, had started amassing the acreage in 1937 with his purchase of the Atlantic Stock Farm, where he raised prize-winning cattle, and over the years he had added several adjacent farms along County Route 537. With its central location in a growing area, its expansive open fields, and its many usable buildings, the Park System designated Dorbrook Farm as a recreation area. Today, after many improvements and added recreation facilities, Dorbrook Recreation Area is the third most-visited park in the Park System.

By using Green Acres matching grants, long-term low interest loans from the new Green Trust Loan Program, and Federal Land and Water

Dorbrook Farm, looking north, 1985.

Monmouth County Park and Recreation Policy Additions

December 2, 1985

Historic and cultural sites and features of countywide significance are in need of preservation, authentic presentation, and interpretation, including elements of historical, archaeological, cultural, and paleontological significance. The County has a responsibility to survey, inventory and assist in historic preservation, restoration, reconstruction, protection, and interpretation of significant County historic and cultural sites and antiquities…for the enjoyment and benefit of existing and future generations.

The County has a responsibility to assist its political subdivisions in meeting the recreational needs of the disabled and other special populations by providing recreation facilities and services that complement those of local governments.

Conservation Funds to acquire Cheeca, Marlu, and Dorbrook Farms, County officials preserved 830 acres of prime farmland and woodland and protected nearly three miles of shoreline on the Swimming River Reservoir. As Jim Truncer noted in the September-October 1985 issue of *Green Heritage,* "County conservationists have given the Freeholders high marks for their foresight and decisive action in the preservation of these open spaces for the citizens of our County." Holmdel Township's subsequent preservation of the adjacent Cross Farm and land along Willow Brook has resulted in more than four and a half miles of protected shoreline on the reservoir.

A place where city kids could come and learn about nature

In another endorsement of the Park System's efforts, the Huber Family decided, 11 years after donating 119 acres of woodlands to create Huber Woods Park in Middletown, to donate the remaining 48 acres of Hans and Catherine Huber's estate, including their house, to expand the park. Mike Huber and his four siblings grew up in the Alpine-style house that his parents built in 1927, and recalled that the family's decision was unanimous. As Mike noted, "I remember getting a letter from my cousin in England saying she would love to see it used as a place where city kids could come and learn about nature and hike around. Everybody seemed to agree this was a great thing because we all loved the place and thought it would be something that the public would love too, and they do."

In their 1985 donation the Hubers specified that the land and buildings should be preserved in their present state and used for light agriculture, passive recreation, and nature study. Park System staff began to hold nature programs in the Huber house, and moved the SPUR therapeutic riding program from Thompson Park into the barns and stables at Huber. As Bruce Gollnick noted in the January-February 1986 issue of *Green Link,* "Riding program participants will have more opportunities to ride through wooded trails, and this (acquisition) will increase our pasture area and provide adequate training rings for the horses. We should all graciously thank the Huber Corporation, since this donation is one dynamite addition."

Left above: Huber House in the 1950s.
Left below: The barns at Huber Woods Park, which became the second home of the SPUR program, pictured in 1999.

Many school groups attend the Park System's annual African American Celebration at the Red Hill Activity Center.

Slavery and Freedom in the Rural North: A History of African Americans in Monmouth County NJ 1665–1865, by Graham Hodges. Initiated by the Park System and published in cooperation with the Friends of the Parks, the book is used by many college history courses.

In December of 1985, the Recreation Commissioners updated their "Park and Recreation Policy" to include recreational opportunities for special populations, preservation of historic sites, and coordination of recreational programs offered throughout the County. Naturalist Gerry Savitz and other Visitor Services staff produced a "Recreation Services Guide" showing existing public recreation resources and identifying additional resources needed for a more "even distribution" of recreation in the County.

In 1986, Jane Clark of the Visitor Services staff initiated the Park System's annual African American History Celebration with performances, lectures and an exhibit on African American history at the Clinton and Mary Heath Wing of the Red Hill Activity Center in Tatum Park. Over the

next several years the program expanded and included an exhibit with artifacts, documents, and photographs of African American culture and early black communities in Monmouth County, some of which remain on display. A companion lecture series eventually led Park System staff and the Friends of the Parks to collaborate on the publication in 1997 of *Slavery and Freedom in the Rural North: A History of African Americans in Monmouth County NJ 1665–1865,* by Graham Hodges.

The County is at a crossroads

Governor Thomas H. Kean and other officials celebrated the 25th anniversary of the Green Acres Program and introduced a sixth Green Acres Bond Act in 1986. The Park System's Annual Report for 1986 highlighted the increasing urgency of preserving open space:

In the last few decades, Monmouth County has changed dramatically from a rustic picturesque area of truck farmers and fishermen, horse breeders and summer vacationers, to a vibrant community of high technology industry, expensive year-round homes, and heavy traffic. As the preserve of open fields, woodland, and waterfront dwindles, the race intensifies between developers and those who realize the importance of preserving scenic beauty and recreational sites for another generation to enjoy, of maintaining breathing space in one of the nation's fastest-growing counties.

With the cyclical and uncertain nature of the Green Acres program, County leaders and private observers considered additional ways to finance land acquisitions. In January of 1987, Freeholder Director Harry Larrison proposed placing a non-binding referendum on the ballot asking voters if they would approve an open space tax—the first in the State—for an Open Space Trust Fund with $4 million annually to preserve land. As Harry told a *Red Bank Register* reporter,

We are fast losing our heritage of open space, forests and fields, and I support spending at least $4 million annually, over and above moneys already raised through bonding, for current acquisitions. However, it's the taxpayer's money and I'm asking the people of Monmouth County to advise the Board of Freeholders on which way they would want us to go on this. The question before the people will essentially be, is it worth $25 or $50 a year to every homeowner to help put the brakes on the overdevelopment of the County and to help save our farmlands and open spaces?

I think the people want us to preserve as much open space as we can. Our little guys and girls 50 years from now deserve a place

An investment that will pay many dividends

"Challenges for the New Year: Open Space,"
Red Bank Register, Editorial, January 2, 1987

Since World War II, the Monmouth County Board of Chosen Freeholders, regardless of which political party was in control, consistently has acted to improve the quality of life for county residents. Primarily because of responsible leadership, the transition from rural community to modern suburb was much smoother here than it was for many counties in New Jersey.

Because Monmouth County leaders historically have made it a priority to preserve the character and beauty of the area, and because it is the preserved character of the county which has made it such a desirable place to live and at the same time helped improve the economy, it therefore would be in the best interests of all residents, including future generations, if the County stays its course and makes every effort to fulfill the goals set forth in its master plan.

The Freeholders should seek out more "creative" ways in which to finance acquisition of open spaces. In their ongoing quest for open space they should focus as well on providing recreation areas in more heavily populated, lower income communities.

Though open space may be costly today, it is an investment that will pay many dividends for Monmouth County in the future.

to play and enjoy themselves. For my part, the additional costs to the County will be more than offset by avoiding the direct and indirect costs of suburban sprawl, including traffic congestion, school, police, sewer, and related costs.

Freeholder Theodore Narozanick told the reporter, "I will wholeheartedly support a referendum. It will give the voters an opportunity to decide whether they want the County to keep developing, or to slow down its speed." Freeholder John Villapiano added, "We have received many questions from residents concerned about the rapid development of the County, and there is a widespread support for the County's purchase of undeveloped areas." Many county residents supported the proposal at a Freeholders' meeting, and the *Asbury Park Press* endorsed it in an editorial, noting, "In a sense, the county is at a crossroads, and important decisions with long-lasting effects must be made soon…To delay consideration of this important question would be to limit severely that County's options, as more and more open land is irretrievably lost."

In assessing development pressures in the "outer ring of suburban counties," the Regional Plan Association noted in its 1987 report, "Where the Pavement Ends," that, "The Region's communities were caught unaware by this explosion of development. Familiar landscapes and important recreation resources—such as golf courses and Boy Scout camps—have been lost. The amount of protected land has nearly doubled in 20 years, but many crucial lands are still threatened with development—including farmlands, valuable wilderness areas, and wetlands which protect vital natural systems. What is happening to the Region's land is clear: more open space needs to be protected throughout the Region, and it must be done quickly because the best land is disappearing fast."

As the November, 1987, election approached, Jim Truncer noted in the September-October 1987 issue of *Green Link*, "As the bulldozer's roar is heard throughout our County, we are not only rapidly running out of open land, but we are running out of time. We have an opportunity to preserve some of our remaining open space if we act in time. Each of us needs to be sure that our citizens understand the importance of the issues they're being asked to decide this November."

Seventy-one percent of Monmouth voters approved the County's non-binding "Park Land Preservation Trust" referendum in 1987 to dedicate $4 million in tax revenues annually to open space acquisition and development, and State voters approved the sixth Green Acres Bond Act as well. County officials subsequently won support from the New Jersey Legislature to implement a county open space tax, and in November, 1989, Monmouth County voters overwhelmingly approved the County's Open Space Tax, the first under the State's newly-enacted enabling legislation. Since that time, numerous counties and municipalities in New Jersey have followed Monmouth's lead in approving local taxes dedicated to preservation of open space and farmland.

Lush fields sandwiched in suburbia

The Neuberger Farm in southern Middletown Township prominently illustrated the intense battle to preserve open space and historic sites in the County. The 129-acre property, flanking both sides of heavily-trafficked Middletown-Lincroft Road, included large barns and a well-preserved farmhouse dating back to the 18th century. Harry and Katherine Neuberger had purchased the farm in 1933 and lived there until their deaths. In 1984, their heirs contracted to sell the farm to Calton Homes Inc., which soon developed a plan to demolish the historic house and build 1,250 housing units on the property.

The Middletown Landmarks Commission had designated the property as a local landmark to protect it, but a lawsuit filed on behalf of the developer resulted in the New Jersey Supreme Court declaring the Township's historic preservation ordinance invalid. Calton's plans included 268 units for low and moderate income residents and, when Middletown designated other sites for subsidized housing to meet its Mt. Laurel obligations, Calton sued the Township under the "builder's remedy" provision of the State's fair housing regulations.

As Calton Homes' lawsuit to develop Neuberger Farm and an adjacent property under the State's Mount Laurel provisions dragged

on, the Vice-President of the company told an *Asbury Park Press* reporter in October, 1989, "The resistance in Middletown is typical of the anti-growth attitude in the state. The difference in Middletown is that the fight is more intense." The reporter described the property being fought over as "one of the largest undeveloped sites remaining in the Township…a 125-acre expanse of lush fields sandwiched in suburbia." Middletown Township Attorney William Dowd told the reporter, "To permit a 1,250 unit development on Neuberger Farm would only exacerbate increasing taxes, traffic snarls, and congestion. The people of Middletown are deeply concerned—and quite rightly—with overdevelopment, which in a nutshell means too much development of any kind."

In response to Middletown's request to preserve the tract, the County began negotiations with Calton to purchase the property. In February 1990, the Freeholders voted to preserve the Neuberger Farm

The Neuberger Farm in 1989, just after a developer demolished a number of large historic barns on the property.

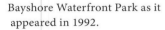

Bayshore Waterfront Park as it
appeared in 1992.

by eminent domain, and the Recreation Commissioners named the
new park Sunnyside Recreation Area, after the farm's historic name.

The frenzy of development in the mid-1980s and the success of the
open space referendum led Park System staff to increase their planning
efforts to identify key parcels of the County's dwindling open space for
preservation. After five years of "putting out fires" and fighting overdevelopment as Middletown Township Planner, Faith Hahn wanted to
focus on long-term planning. As she recalled, "I knew Spence Wickham
from the Park System's numerous projects in Middletown, and one day
I mentioned to him that I was ready for a change. He said, 'We're working on a new open space plan and we really could use someone with
your skills.' They wanted to have a better, closer working relationship
with municipalities, and I had the advantages and understanding of
that perspective and Spence offered me a job."

Faith joined the Park System's Acquisition and Design staff as principal planner in early 1988 and started working on the inventory and
mapping project that was underway to identify recreational and natu-

ral resources throughout the County. That spring the Acquisition and
Design staff organized a countywide "Green Spaces, Livable Places"
conference, with help from the Monmouth Conservation Foundation,
for local officials, developers, and concerned individuals to explore
ways of combining development with protection of open space and
natural resources.

County Planning Director Charles Pike's goal in the 1960 "Recreation
Study and Plan" to create a County park on the Bayshore came to
fruition in 1988 with the start of Bayshore Waterfront Park in the Port
Monmouth section of Middletown Township. Because the land in this
area consisted primarily of small lots, the creation of Bayshore Waterfront Park has been unique in the Park System. Beginning with an 8.4
acre donation from the Conservation Fund in 1988, the Park System's
land acquisition staff has gradually acquired more than 90 lots as they
became available and has consolidated them into the 226-acre Park.
The lots included disturbed urban shoreline and wetlands, and the Park
System has gradually returned this environmentally-significant land

to its undeveloped condition for public park use. The growing Park quickly became a favorite spot for beachcombing, fishing and enjoying the spectacular waterfront views. In 1998, the Park System exchanged land with Middletown Township to add 12 acres of open space to the Park, including a fishing pier and the historic Seabrook-Wilson House overlooking Sandy Hook Bay.

A priority goal identified in the 1970 "Open Space Plan" to protect stream corridors got a big boost in 1988 as the Park System started a multi-year effort to preserve more land along the Crosswicks Creek in Upper Freehold Township. Thanks to Joanne and Ed Mullen's 36-acre donation of Walnford in 1979, and to the Green Acres program, County officials had already preserved over 200 acres along the stream valley to protect Walnford and its historic rural setting.

The new effort reflected a growing trend to create greenways in order protect key stream corridors from the impact of development. Through purchases, farmland preservation, and conservation easements, the County, the Green Acres Program, the Farmland Preservation Program, the Township of Upper Freehold, the N.J. Conservation Foundation, and the Monmouth Conservation Foundation have collectively preserved more than 4,000 acres along Crosswicks Creek. Of the total, the Park System has acquired 1,479 acres in the Crosswicks Creek Greenway, making it the second largest County Park after Turkey Swamp Park.

The preferable choice

Another water supply initiative was realized in 1988 with the NJ Water Supply Authority's lease agreement with the County for recreational use of 1,052 acres around the Manasquan Reservoir in the Oak Glen area of Howell Township. Charles Pike had recommended in the 1960 "Recreation Study and Plan" that the Manasquan River be preserved for water supply "with full utilization of its recreational potential," and the State's Manasquan River Reservoir Land Use Task Force had concluded in the mid-1980s that fishing, boating with small motors, and hiking, riding and bicycling on a perimeter trail would be compatible with the reservoir. The Task Force recommended preserving a buffer zone of open space around the reservoir for habitat protection and nature study, and suggested consideration of a "nature center" as well. After reviewing recreational management options for the reservoir, the Task Force members unanimously concluded that the Monmouth County Park System was "the preferable choice."

The Recreation Commissioners began a new era of leadership in early 1989 by electing Adeline "Addy" Lubkert as Chairman. The Freeholders appointed Mrs. Lubkert to the Board in 1982, where she served as Vice Chairman from 1986–1989 and as Chairman until her retirement from the Board in 2007. Adeline Lubkert is the longest-serving Commissioner in Park System history, with 25 years of service.

By the end of the 1980s, the Park System had created 22 parks with 6,495 acres of open space and recreational facilities, and annual visitation had surpassed 2.5 million people.

ADELINE HOLMES LUBKERT

It's really that good

I was born in the house where I live and my father, John Holmes, farmed the land. He grew mostly potatoes and had a couple of milk cows. Both of my grandmothers lived in the center of Holmdel Village and I went to a one room school there that is now town hall. I went on to Red Bank High School and then to Goucher College in Baltimore.

When I was growing up, there was a lot more open space back then and never a thought that it would be anything but open space. Later on, a lot of people around here still thought we didn't need parks. One of the interesting things to me was that there was a group of people who were very interested in having a park system that would take care of everybody and it would be all over the County. They wanted to provide the right kind of things for the people that needed them, and I got interested in that. Later people finally got to realize that you better save land while you can or it will be gone. When people think that way, then things get accomplished.

As far as I'm concerned, the people in the Park System—all the employees, the Friends of the Parks, the volunteers—the way they work and see what has to be done, I think they deserve all the credit in the world. The Park System in Monmouth County is the best around, and I mean in all of the United States. It's really that good. I just hope it keeps on and I think it will.

A truly outstanding job

AS THE 1990s began, the Park System was poised for a major surge in both land acquisition and visitation. The approval of the 1989 Green Acres Bond Act and the County Open Space Referendum had together created an unprecedented amount of open space and recreation funding, and County leaders and employees were prepared to move quickly to take advantage of it. They would preserve nearly 5,000 acres and create 12 new parks in the 1990s, but the preserved land was only about 10% of the open space that would be lost to development during that decade.

In early 1989, after members of the Park System's Open Space Planning Team had completed mapping the County's land use and natural and cultural resources, they took their findings on the road and met with individual municipalities over the course of several months. Energized by the enthusiastic support of local officials for an aggressive land preservation program, the Planning Team, led by Park System planner Faith Hahn, prepared an ambitious draft plan that was warmly received at a series of six public meetings held throughout the county in January, 1990. In these public presentations, members of the Team emphasized that, as the competition for land grew, it was critical to develop new strategies and partnerships to gain control of key parcels before development swallowed them up.

The Planning Team's "Park, Recreation and Open Space Plan" proclaimed that "Open space is an element of the public infrastructure, which, like bridges, schools, and water lines, must be provided and maintained to sustain the rest of the community." While reflecting the generalized goals and policies of the Park System's earlier plans, the "Park, Recreation and Open Space Plan" defined open space as a complex and connected environmental system of plant and animal habitats, water resources, and human land uses as farms, fisheries, forests, recreation areas, and historic and cultural sites. It also embraced the understanding that open spaces often require special management for public health and safety, such as floodplains, watersheds, and reservoirs for water quality and preserved areas for air quality, and that open spaces are important to the image of a community because of their strong visual impact and their relationship to the surrounding built environment.

The "Park, Recreation and Open Space Plan" called for New Jersey officials to develop a statewide open space strategy and for the County and its municipalities to integrate open space objectives into their

Opposite: Historic Walnford.

planning, operating, and regulatory activities. It also emphasized the County's role in providing technical support to municipalities and in stimulating cooperative efforts. On private land, the Plan encouraged new strategies and incentives to protect natural resources and provide public access where possible. For acquisitions, the Plan targeted areas with special natural features, greenways for trails and water protection, recreation areas for sports and riding, golf courses, additions to existing parks, and the development of new parks in the coastal, Bayshore, and Marlboro/Manalapan/Millstone areas.

While the earlier plans had general acquisition goals, the Plan identified specific additions totaling more than 1,700 acres to 13 of the Park System's 22 parks. These additions included 230 acres for Clayton Park, 130 for Walnford, 410 for Howell Park and the Manasquan Reservoir, 300 for Turkey Swamp Park, 150 for Dorbrook Recreation Area, 200 for Huber Woods Park, and 105 for Shark River Park. The Plan also identified 10 new park and golf course sites, including Perrineville Lake in Millstone as a 500-acre regional park, Charleston Springs in Millstone as a 980-acre golf course, Big Brook in Marlboro as a 660-acre regional

All of these things are possible in Monmouth County

"Park, Recreation and Open Space Plan," 1991

Imagine beaches, nature preserves, ball fields, and marinas permanently protected from development and open to the public.

Imagine streams, ponds, and rivers whose banks are accessible to the public, whose waters are stocked with fish, and which are protected from erosion and flooding by sensitive land practices.

Imagine a trail near your home where you can walk for leisure or exercise, or where your child can ride a bike safely to school.

Imagine a public golf course with a waiting time of only 15 minutes.

Imagine showing your grandchildren the farm where you were raised or the woods where you played as a youngster, instead of telling them what was there before the houses.

This is no fantasy...all of these things are possible in Monmouth County. It is we, not some untamable

beast, who control the future of the County, and the choice of what the future will be is ours.

We can mourn the way conventional subdivisions consume treasured landscapes, or we can encourage creative development by rewriting our zoning ordinances, require and accept conservation and scenic easements, and experiment with innovative preservation techniques such as transfer of development rights.

We can claim that the job of preserving open space and improving our recreational facilities is too big and not even try, or we can enlist the aid of civic groups and the sponsorship of corporations and tackle the job together.

The County has chosen to take an active role in deciding our open space future...but implementation of the plan will require a cooperative effort.

Crosswicks Creek Greenway, Upper Freehold Township.

The Park System's Open Space Planning Team in 1992. Seated: Andrew Coeyman, Faith Hahn, and Tom Collins. Standing: Robin Ostrowski, Joseph Sardonia, Ken Thoman, Andrew North, Gail Hunton, and Francesca Martone.

park, Wolf Hill in Oceanport as a 90-acre regional recreation area, and Fisherman's Cove in Manasquan as a 60-acre special use area.

The Plan called for the State to add 1,070 acres to its Turkey Swamp Wildlife Management Area and 368 acres to Monmouth Battlefield. It specified 35 greenways, bikeways, and trails totaling 238 miles plus nine conservation areas with more than 2,100 acres to be created or protected through State, County, and municipal acquisitions, easements, and regulations.

In recognition of the Planning Team's accomplishments, Jim Truncer wrote in the March-April, 1990 *Green Link*, "Through the efforts of the staff in the Acquisition and Design Department, our County will be better prepared to meet the quality-of-life concerns of our citizens as our County continues to grow and change. My hat's off to the open space planning staff for a truly outstanding job."

The Park System's efforts to proceed quickly with one key project in the "Park, Recreation and Open Space Plan"—the Manasquan River Greenway—ran into some public opposition. With the long-awaited Manasquan Reservoir nearing completion, the staff wanted to preserve land along the upstream corridor to protect this key potable water supply as much as possible. At the initial meetings with Howell and Freehold Townships in 1989, the local officials had lauded the creation of the Greenway as complementing their own master plans. However, when Park System acquisition staff began to contact property owners in the project area, rumors circulated that that the County would actively use eminent domain to create the Greenway. In a November, 1989, article with the headline "Greenway proposal has some seeing red," the *Asbury Park Press* noted that one property owner claimed "he's got nothing against protecting the Manasquan River, which runs behind his property in Howell Township. But he and many of his neighbors object to the county forcing them to sell some of their land to extend public access along the river's banks, which they say will make their homes and farm animals more vulnerable to abuse."

When Park System staff held a public meeting at Howell High School in March, 1990, about the proposed Greenway, about 150 people attended and many expressed concerns about the County's potential condemnation of their land. The staff described the Greenway as a long-term project and stressed the County's preference for dealing with land owners who were interested in having their properties appraised for possible sale. By the end of 1990, the Park System had purchased three parcels totaling 17 acres along the river to start the

Manasquan River Greenway. Over the next 19 years, the Park System staff expanded the Greenway to 338 acres. Of the total 39 properties acquired, only four acquisitions have involved eminent domain.

To advance another project proposed in the "Park, Recreation, and Open Space Plan," in June of 1990 the Park System used County Open Space Trust funds to acquire the 204-acre former Bobbink Nursery in Millstone Township, identified in the Plan as Charleston Springs, a potential golf course site to serve the western portion of the County. Two years later, the Park System acquired the adjacent 383-acre Bulk Nursery property and the sellers donated an additional 34 acres, bringing the Charleston Springs golf course site to 621 acres.

The County Planning Board and the Recreation Commissioners adopted the "Park, Recreation and Open Space Plan" in the summer of 1991. The N.J. Chapter of the American Planning Association gave the Park System its annual Outstanding Environmental Achievement Award for the Plan in 1992.

Virtually irreplaceable in this developed region

As an example of the governmental cooperation encouraged by the "Park, Recreation and Open Space Plan," the Park System assumed management of the Bayshore rail corridor between Aberdeen and Atlantic Highlands in 1990 and created the Henry Hudson Trail, the County's first rail-trail. The Central Railroad of New Jersey had built this Seashore Branch line in the late 19th century to haul freight from northern Monmouth industries and farms and to transport commuters and tourists traveling to towns along the Bayshore and the ocean. Conrail took over the service but eventually discontinued it, and in the 1980s it tried to sell portions of the nine-mile right-of-way. After a lawsuit blocked the sales, the County used a State grant to purchase the right-of-way for a possible light rail line in the future.

With the agreement of Bayshore towns, the Park System converted the right-of-way into a recreational trail that travels through communities, across streams and salt marsh, and over local streets where people can access the trail. After cleaning up what had been a litter-strewn and overgrown abandoned corridor, removing over 70 encroachments, and improving over 30 street crossings, Park System staff opened portions of the Henry Hudson Trail starting in 1992. They used funding from a Federal ISTEA transportation enhancement grant to renovate or replace 11 bridges and to install signage along the entire trail.

County officials and Park System employees celebrated the opening of nine miles of the Henry Hudson Trail on National Trails Day in June, 1995. The trail links the communities of Atlantic Highlands, Middletown, Keansburg, Union Beach, Hazlet, Keyport, and Aberdeen. Hikers, bikers, and joggers could travel from Atlantic Highlands to just east of the Garden State Parkway, with bridge crossings providing open views of stream corridors, tidal wetlands, and Sandy Hook Bay. The trail soon became particularly popular with Bayshore residents and, as *Green*

Above: The Park System acquired Bulk Nursery in Millstone Township in 1992 to create Charleston Springs Golf Course.

Below: The abandoned Central Railroad of New Jersey rail corridor across Chingarora Creek in 1989, prior to improvements to create the Henry Hudson Trail.

Heritage noted in its June-July, 1995 issue, this resource is "virtually irreplaceable in this developed region." The Park System's success in developing and managing this first trail has helped generate political and public support for additional trail projects.

Unparalleled in Monmouth County

In another example of inter-governmental collaboration, the Park System assumed management of the public use of the State's new Manasquan Reservoir in Howell Township, the first step in realizing the long-held vision to develop the recreational potential of the reservoir. After the dam was completed, people patiently awaited the months-long filling of the four billion-gallon reservoir, eager to see what the site would look like and to use it for fishing, boating, and hiking. As the reservoir filled up in early 1990, the *Asbury Park Press* noted, "Completion of the project will be a momentous achievement for the hundreds of people who have worked on it during the years."

As the Park System prepared to open the Manasquan Reservoir in September, 1990, Tom Fobes, the park manager, told an *Asbury Park Press* reporter, "It's a new and different facility, and it has tons of wildlife. We're excited to be here. I think it's going to be one of the best facili-

Below left: Sailing Camp on the Manasquan Reservoir.

Above right: Manasquan Reservoir Visitor Center.

ties we have." The Park System opened the Reservoir in the fall of 1990 with 282 acres of recreation land around the 770-acre lake, including a partially-completed perimeter trail, several parking areas, and two boat launch ramps on the southern shore. As construction crews worked on a new maintenance building, Park System staff developed plans for a Visitor Center and boating facility on the south shore and an Environmental Center on the west shore.

As Faith Hahn noted in the October 1990 issue of *Open Spaces, Livable Places*, the Park System's planning newsletter, the agreement between the N.J. Water Supply Authority and the Park System is "a prime example of how the coordination of programs and projects among public agencies can advance important open space objectives at little cost to the taxpayer. Thus, the public acquisition and development of one site yields a new source of potable water, spares aquifers throughout the County from depletion from overuse, and provides an opportunity for freshwater recreation unparalleled in Monmouth County."

In its first full year of operation in 1991, the Manasquan Reservoir attracted over 128,000 visitors and recorded more than 2,000 boat launchings. Three years later, the Freeholders and Recreation Commissioners opened an 8,000 square foot Visitor Center, fishing pier, and boating facility at the Reservoir. The N.J. Recreation and Park Association gave the Park System its Kinsey Award in recognition of the Visitor Center's design excellence.

A month after opening the reservoir in 1990, the Freeholders added another prime water recreation property to the Park System with the acquisition of the 10-acre Gateway Marina in Port Monmouth on the Bayshore. Purchased with Green Acres funding, the property included a fuel dock, floating docks with slips for 140 boats, storage racks for 80 boats, a boat shop, marina equipment, and some beachfront. The Park System had targeted it for acquisition back in 1984 when its Monmouth County Marina Study predicted a steep decline in rental boat

slips as the County's marinas succumbed to waterfront housing developments. The Recreation Commissioners named it the Monmouth Cove Marina.

We have only one environment, we'd better protect it

In 1990, more than 500 volunteers contributed over 14,500 hours of work to park maintenance and programs. The remarkable range of volunteers' activities included giving tours, planting gardens, interpreting 1890s rural living history at Longstreet Farm, assisting with therapeutic recreation and equestrian programs for individuals with special needs, clearing and establishing trails, and producing summer theater. Many people and businesses donated artifacts, art objects, plant materials, and educational and recreational supplies and equipment, and individuals and organizations also contributed funds to specific programs or improvement projects.

To enable people to help the Park System in other ways, Jim Truncer and several staff members worked with county residents Frank McDonough, Joanne Mullen, Daniel Ward Seitz, and other supporters in 1991 to establish the Friends of the Parks as a non-profit organization dedicated to enhancing Park System activities, facilities, and services. To introduce people to the new Friends' organization, McDonough, an attorney in Red Bank, sponsored a 'Friends-Maker' walk around the undeveloped Weltz Park in Ocean Township, and Joanne Mullen sponsored a tour of Walnford, which she and her husband Ed had donated to the Park System in 1979. Daniel Ward Seitz, a descendant of the Hartshorne family, sponsored a 'Friends-Maker' walk through Hartshorne Woods Park, where Frank McDonough told the group, "I come from Ocean Township, which is 95% built up, and I know how very important it is to preserve these woods intact."

The 22 founding members expanded the Friends of the Parks to 129 members in their first year and raised $15,000 through membership fees, donations, and events such as the raffle of a Victorian Dinner at Longstreet Farm in Holmdel Park to support an exhibit in the farmhouse. They established specific funds for projects and equipment in Turkey Swamp, Hartshorne Woods, Huber Woods, and Seven Presidents Parks, and a Recreation Scholarships Fund that sponsored 483 participants from low-income urban areas to attend recreational programs in County Parks. The Friends also sponsored a Rails-to-Trails Celebration along the Henry Hudson Trail, where McDonough told the participants, "We have only one environment and we'd better protect it."

Friends of the Parks Board 1993: (seated from left) John Linney, Frank McDonough, Jim Truncer, Joanne Mullen; (standing from left) Edward P. Pitts, Carol Tomson, Daniel Ward Seitz, Joan Rechnitz, Dominick Cerrato.

In 1993, the Friends held the first Friends of the Parks Golf Tournament at Hominy Hill Golf Course. Over the years this tournament has become a popular tradition and the group's signature fundraising event. In the nearly two decades since its founding, the Friends organization has raised over $2.5 million for many different projects that have immeasurably enhanced both the parks and the experiences of people who use them.

To recognize the increasing value of the volunteers, the Friends of the Parks started giving "Volunteers in Parks" awards in 1994 to people who contributed more than 500 hours of "their time, talent, and energy." That year, Friends Chairman Daniel Ward Seitz awarded special recognition to five volunteers who had each contributed more than 1,000 hours to facilities or programs such as historic interpretation at Longstreet Farm, the gardens at Deep Cut, and therapeutic riding at Huber Woods Park.

By the end of the 1990s decade, over 1,300 people were annually donating nearly 40,000 hours of their time, effort, and expertise volunteering in Monmouth County Parks and recreation programs. The volunteer activities had expanded to teaching about nature, planting dune grass and over 1,200 tree seedlings, helping SPUR (Special People United to Ride) with therapeutic riding programs, extensive gardening at Deep Cut Gardens and Thompson Park, and helping with many other projects and events. From the beginning of the volunteer program in 1976 through the end of the 1990s, over 10,000 generous

Master Gardener volunteers helped plant the restored parterre at Deep Cut Gardens.

In early 1991, Andy Coeyman became Supervisor of the Land Preservation Office, where he benefited greatly from having already worked for the Park System for twelve years as a naturalist and for five years in the land acquisition office. A self-described 'Army brat' born at Ft. Monmouth in Oceanport, Andy graduated from Monmouth College (now Monmouth University), where he studied biology. In the nearly two decades that he has supervised land preservation, the Park System has

individuals had donated an incredible 250,000 hours. Friends of the Parks presented volunteer service awards to eight individuals in 1999 who had each contributed more than 1,000 hours.

Friends of the Parks Mission – First Annual Report 1992

To increase the Park System's value through donations of services, property, financial assistance, scholarships, and coordination of volunteer activities.

To increase existing resources through funding beautification, restoration, and limited capital improvement projects.

To improve and expand programs.

To enhance the delivery of park services to groups with special needs.

To assist local groups which provide direct assistance to particular parks and activities.

To solicit and hold money and property from grants, gifts, bequests, and contributions.

ANDREW COEYMAN

For the kids of the future

At some point in college, I wanted to work outdoors with wildlife. I first encountered the MCPS in 1972 during an ecology class field trip to Thompson Park. Gerry Savitz showed us the animal collection, then housed in the Rec Barn, and I was very impressed with Gerry. I landed a job as naturalist in 1974, and what really made it great was working with the naturalists and interpreters, Howard Wikoff, Nick Fiorillo, Bob Henschel, Doug Krampert and Gerry, with Tom Kellers at the top, and later Pat Contreras and Patty O'Rourke. They all had different interests, and I was like a sponge, and soaked up a lot of what they knew. It was a great job because I got paid to learn about the parks and the nature of the County and then got to pass it on to park visitors and students.

I was brought over to the planning team in November, 1986, and took over land acquisition in February, 1991. The Open Space Plan and Open Space Tax came in about the same time and told us what project areas to work on and gave us the money to buy the properties as they became available. We have acquired thousands of acres since then.

It has been a great career, and I am indeed fortunate to work here. Working with great people has also made my job wonderful. I guess my zeal for land preservation comes from hunting, fishing, and camping as a kid in Wall, and seeing beloved spots turn into houses. If we can preserve such places, then they will always be there for the kids of the future. I just hope that we can continue buying land and establishing parks and that the MCPS lasts for a thousand years or more.

preserved thousands of acres. As he told his colleague Fran Martone in 1992, "People won't remember you and me in a hundred years, but they'll see what we did."

On Memorial Day Weekend of 1992, County and Park System officials celebrated the opening of the Environmental Center and new trails in Huber Woods Park. More than 50 Park System staff members from multiple departments collaborated on the projects, demonstrating their creativity and skills in a variety of disciplines. Designers, planners, naturalists, carpenters, and other Park employees renovated the former Huber house for the Environmental Center and created exhibits interpreting the history and ecology of the Park.

Ken Thoman, Park System Ecologist, developed the trails plan for the Park and collaborated with Assistant Superintendent Lee Homyock, Principal Park Ranger Ed Orr, and other rangers and volunteers to improve the existing trails and create new ones for a variety of hiking and riding experiences. They created a Nature Loop trail as a linear "outdoor classroom" to inform visitors about the nearby habitats, and an accessible Discovery Path with native plants to attract birds for bird-watching. Ken and other staff members also converted areas of turf and former pasture into a wildlife meadow and fields of native grasses.

The National Association of Park and Recreation Officials recognized the Park System's achievement at Huber Woods with its 1993 Award of Excellence for design and development, noting that the Environmental Center and outdoor improvements had transformed the once private estate into a premier regional park.

With the quick success of the trails at Huber Woods Park, Ken developed a "Park Trails Program" for upgrading and maintaining trails in other County parks. The Program included developing standards for different types of trails: from short and flat groomed trails for casual hikers, to long and steep trails with rough surfaces for hikers and bicyclists who prefer moderate or challenging levels of difficulty.

With the strong public support for open space in Monmouth County and all around the State, New Jersey voters in November of 1992 overwhelmingly approved the eighth Green Acres Bond Act for $200 million for open space acquisition, farmland preservation, and historic preservation. The Park System received two significant historic preservation matching grants through the N.J. Historic Trust funded by this Green Acres Bond Act and the prior one. The Trust awarded a $1 million grant from the 1989 Bond Act for restoration of the grist mill, colonial house, and main barns at Walnford, and a $110,000 grant from the 1992 Bond

Below left: Huber Woods Environmental Center, 1996.

Below right: Trails volunteers at Huber Woods, 2009. From the start of the Park Trails Program in 1993, volunteers have been instrumental in its implementation. Citizens committed to enhancing the ecology of the parks worked on the Huber trails in the 1990s and continue to volunteer today.

The Nomoco Activity Area at Turkey Swamp Park, formerly Camp Nomoco, offers group camping facilities amidst extensive woodlands.

Act for the restoration of the 1792 Dutch Barn that is the centerpiece of the historic farm complex at Longstreet Farm. The Trust later awarded the Park System supplemental grants for both sites totaling $676,358. By leveraging County funds, these grants enabled the Park System to undertake the historically-appropriate restoration that these significant buildings deserved.

To a buyer who cares more about nature

In May of 1993, the Park System acquired Camp Nomoco from the Monmouth Council of Girl Scouts to add it to Turkey Swamp Park, and recreation staff members started nature and swimming programs there just a few months later. The Council had operated the 303-acre camp since 1947 and, over the years thousands of girls had enjoyed day and overnight visits at its 56-acre campground, but camping had become less popular for girls and registration had declined.

The Council trustees were determined to sell the camp, as a *Wall Herald* reporter noted, to "a buyer who cares more about nature and a pristine environment than about developing the land." Park System staff saw the Nomoco acquisition as a logical addition to Turkey Swamp Park because it helped protect the Metedeconk River watershed while converting a private camping facility into a public one.

In addition to Camp Nomoco, the Park System has preserved four

other private camps through easements: the Quail Hill Boy Scout Reservation in Manalapan, Camp Sacajawea in Howell, YMCA Camp Arrowhead in Marlboro, and YMCA Camp Topanemus in Millstone.

In 1994, the Commission for Accreditation of Park and Recreation Agencies (CAPRA) awarded its first-ever national accreditation to the Monmouth County Park System. CAPRA developed the national accreditation program to recognize agencies that meet the highest level of professional standards in 10 categories: agency authority, planning, organization and administration, human resources, finance, program and services management, facility and land use management, security and public safety, risk management, and evaluation and research. In the 1994 Park System Annual Report, Freeholder Ted Narozanick said about CAPRA's accreditation, "This pat on the back, like that which our Park System employees already receive from visitors to the parks, is more evidence that employees are helping to maintain a top-rate organization." The Park System has received CAPRA's reaccreditation every five years since 1994.

Commission for Accreditation of Park and Recreation Agencies

First National Accreditation, Monmouth County Park System, 1994

The Acquisition and Planning Department exceeded national standards…and the personnel were well trained, experienced, well versed and capable of working with the taxpayers, homeowners, and general public.

The Monmouth County Park System is exceptionally well organized and administered. Despite budget crunches, this agency has been able to provide adequate support services in its divisions and departments. It has clearly established lines and levels of responsibility. A strong sense of positive and happy morale is very much evidenced.

The visitor team was very favorably impressed with the high quality of achievements and the amount of work being performed by the Board, staff, and all employees with whom we came in contact. We found nothing but excellent cooperation, a friendly spirit of interest, helpfulness, and hospitality.

Marvelous enthusiasm

The Park System hosted the U.S. Golf Association's 19th U.S. Women's Amateur Public Links Championship at Hominy Hill Golf Course in June, 1995. The Women's Championship is a showcase for the finest amateur women public links golfers, and U.S.G.A. officials wanted a particularly memorable event that year because the Association was celebrating its 100th anniversary. The Park System opened the seven-day Centennial Championship, as the U.S.G.A. dubbed the event, free of charge to the public, and hundreds of spectators came to observe golfers from 33 states.

In thanking the Park System for its efforts, as *Green Link* reported in September-October, 1995, the U.S.G.A. event chairwoman wrote, "The Centennial Championship was the finest one of all the 19 we've had. From the golf course itself, to the staff at Hominy Hill, to the heads of all the committees, everything was absolutely superb. It was all so perfect – the clubhouse, the merchandise, the caddies, the staff. I wish we could bottle this championship for the future because the combination was ideal." As one of the tournament players wrote to the Park System, "Thank you all for the use of your great course and for your marvelous enthusiasm in supporting the tournament. None of the players will ever forget it."

While Park System officials welcomed the acknowledgements from tournament players, they were particularly gratified that golfers of all skill levels were enthusiastically patronizing their four golf courses. In their 1995 Annual Report, Park System staff noted, "Because of the popularity of Monmouth County's golf courses, there can be as many as 35,000 attempts to access the Park System reservation service's 16 phone lines during the first half hour of tee time availability. With 180,000 rounds of golf played yearly on County courses, demand for tee times is extremely high." Today, the Park System utilizes a computerized reservation system that enables golfers to reserve tee times easily.

With this considerable demand, the Recreation Commissioners decided to proceed with the development of the Charleston Springs Golf Course in Millstone Township. Under the leadership of Supervising Landscape Architect Joe Sardonia and Golf Courses General Manager Dave Pease, a team of Park System staff developed environmental objectives for the course's design, construction, and management, including wetlands and habitat areas for native plants and animals and minimizing the use of water, fertilizers, and pesticides.

The Park System engaged nationally-known golf course architects Cornish, Silva and Mungeam of Uxbridge, Massachusetts, to design two 18-hole regulation golf courses for Charleston Springs, with a golf center, putting green, practice range, plus 70 acres of passive recreation. The architects designed a "links-style" North Course, with few trees and an expanse of native grasses and water features with aquatic habitats, and complemented it with "parkland-style" South Course, with tree-lined fairways and water features built to collect and filter runoff water for supplemental irrigation.

The North Course at Charleston Springs opened for limited play six months ahead of schedule in the fall of 1998, and Golf Ranger Bob Giolotto reported, "Ninety-eight percent of the golfers are loving the course. They give it rave reviews and can't wait to play here again." The course's environmental design has generated many positive comments.

In the summer of 1995, the County moved forward with the preservation of one of the last large parcels along Monmouth County's

Buffer of native wetlands plants on Charleston Springs Golf Course. The design of the course helps protect natural resources while providing an aesthetically pleasing course for people to golf, goals supported by a National Golf Foundation survey which revealed that, "getting outdoors and reconnecting with nature were among the top reasons why people play golf."

Above: Fisherman's Cove, 1992.

Right: Youth Tournament at Bel-Aire Golf Course, 2008. The Park System is "growing the game" by expanding access and instruction at county golf courses for all ages and abilities.

Atlantic shoreline, with the acquisition of 35 acres at the mouth of the Manasquan River known as Fisherman's Cove. While much of the site consists of tidelands, the acquisition preserved 15 acres that had been zoned for high-density housing, thus concluding years of local opposition to potential development. With the support of local preservation advocates, the Park System designated the site as the Fisherman's Cove Conservation Area. Park System staff renovated a former bait and tackle shop on the site and started offering environmental education programs there focused on the Manasquan tidelands.

We are indeed fortunate

New Jersey voters approved the ninth Green Acres Bond Act in November, 1995, providing $250 million for open space preservation, recreation facilities, farmland preservation, and historic preservation. Since the first Green Acres Bond Act in 1991, $1.4 billion in Green Acres, farmland, and historic preservation matching grants had helped to preserve over 779,000 acres, to develop numerous recreation facilities, and to restore many important historic sites all around New Jersey.

A year later, in November, 1996, Monmouth residents voted by a 3 to 1 margin to increase the County's open space tax from the $4 million in annual funding approved in 1987 to $10 million, with $8 million for preserving land and $2 million for park improvements. Jim Truncer wrote to the staff in the November-December, 1996 *Green Link*, "We are indeed fortunate to have such dedicated citizens who are interested in their Park System and the preservation of open space in our County. Only with a quality organization of dedicated people doing an outstanding job, day in and day out, are we able to receive the support we need from our voters. I believe the County Open Space Referendum was as much a referendum on the Park System as on increased County open space funding. Thanks to all of you for your hard work, interest, and dedication in making your Park System worthy of voters' support."

In the next two years, the additional Green Acres and Open Space Tax funding enabled the Park System to acquire its fifth golf course and create three parks proposed in the 1991 "Park, Recreation and Open Space Plan." The Freeholders accepted an offer in 1997 from the owners of the 78-acre Bel-Aire Golf Course in Wall Township to sell it to the County. The 30-year-old "executive style" course was popular with beginners and senior citizens who preferred its shorter greens and fairways to those of regulation-size courses. The acquisition preserved open space along a major highway in a rapidly developing area and provided a public golf course for a segment of the market that the Park System was not serving in southeastern Monmouth County.

The Park System passed the 10,000-acre milestone in August, 1997, when the Freeholders acquired 378 acres of Marlboro State Hospital land from the State. With its open space, wetlands, and nearly a mile of frontage along Big Brook—a tributary of the Swimming River—the site had considerable conservation value, and Marlboro Township officials had long urged the Park System to preserve it. The Recreation Commissioners named the new site Big Brook Park. A month later, the Freeholders bought the 91-acre Wolf Hill Farm in Oceanport from the N.J. Sports and Exposition Authority. The Recreation Commissioners named it the Wolf Hill Recreation Area because of its suitability for active recreation in a populated portion of the County. The County added a third new park site in June of 1998 with the purchase of 109 acres along De-Bois Creek and Route 33 in Freehold Township, named the DeBois Creek Recreation Area.

In response to a 1996 survey of recreational interests in the County, the Park System significantly expanded facilities at two large parks in 1997 to serve a variety of recreational needs. Since opening the Dorbrook Recreation Area with 381 acres in 1985, the Park System had expanded it to over 520 acres. In 1997, Park System staff opened a new Activity Center with additional indoor space for therapeutic recreation summer camps, sports and fitness programs, and cultural activities. The Park System also upgraded Dorbrook's outdoor facilities, including its swimming pools, courts, playing fields, and playgrounds, and it added an in-line skating rink.

In 1997 the Park System also opened a new 11,000 square foot Creative Arts Center in a converted dairy barn at Thompson Park for pottery and ceramics and other crafts classes. Visitor Services staff presented more than 4,000 programs and recreational activities throughout the Park System in 1997. With financial assistance from the Friends of the Parks, Recreation Assistance Program staff provided activities for thousands of economically disadvantaged County residents.

Above: Dorbrook Recreation Area, 2003.

Right: Pottery class, Creative Arts Center. The Creative Arts Center currently offers approximately 400 classes a year in a wide variety of arts and crafts.

A once-in-a-lifetime opportunity

In October of 1997, County officials opened Historic Walnford in Upper Freehold Township and marked the 225th anniversary of Richard Waln's purchase of the farm and gristmill there. Hundreds of people turned out to enjoy Walnford's historic setting and the restored grist mill, colonial house, and farm buildings. After Ed and Joanne Mullen had donated Walnford to the County in 1979, Park System staff extensively researched the property and developed restoration and interpretive plans for this National Register site, with the assistance of a consulting millwright, archaeologists, historic architects, historic interiors specialists, and exhibit designers.

Noting the project's team effort, Park System Historic Preservation Specialist Gail Hunton, who led the site restoration, told a reporter, "It's really a thrill to be involved with a process like this. It's a once-in-a-lifetime opportunity. Rather than focusing on one particular period of time, our tours of Walnford will explain how it has evolved over its 250-year history."

Expanding on earlier initiatives to allow natural processes to prevail on the park landscapes, Park System Ecologist Ken Thoman worked with park managers to establish a systemwide Field Maintenance Program in 1998 to improve their stewardship of the thousands of acres of fields in the parks. The staff members inventoried and classified various types of fields according to dominant plants, habitat, and use and developed field maintenance plans for each type that prescribed strat-

Above: The Timberbrook Triathlon at the Manasquan Reservoir, first held in 1995.

Right: Walnford Day, 2000. Every October since the opening of Historic Walnford in 1997, the Park System hosts Walnford Day with special activities and demonstrations.

Field Management - 2001

As the Park System has acquired land over the decades, stewardship of the varied resources within the parks has become increasingly important. The thousands of acres of fields within the parks provide a major vegetative cover and habitat for birds, animals, and insects. They buffer adjacent streams, contribute to the visual character and variety of the parks, and support a range of uses.

Open Play Areas have turf grasses for lawns and athletic use.

Grassy Fields are generally composed of cool season grasses that are allowed to grow with minimal mowing to resemble old-fashioned hay fields, or native warm season grasses that more resemble native prairie.

Agricultural Fields are planted with traditional crops such as corn or soybeans.

Old Fields are composed of herbaceous plants and grasses often dominated by goldenrods, or a mix of warm season grasses and wildflowers.

Shrublands are early succession trees and shrubs.

Barrens have sparse or intermittent vegetation, such as beaches, disturbed areas, and farm fields.

Management standards for enhancing native plant and animal communities, minimizing maintenance, and providing appropriate recreational access to a variety of sites are:

Athletic— athletic fields and golf courses with seeding and irrigation to maintain high-quality turf under demanding conditions; grass height maintained at 2 1/2 - 3 inches; aeration, weed control, fertilizer.

Formal/turf areas—developed and high-visitation areas, often with formal or open play; grass height maintained at 3 - 4 1/2 inches; aeration, weed control, seeding, and fertilizer applied as needed to maintain quality turf during April through October; often not irrigated.

Grassy Field—areas with low traffic and open play; cool season grasses mowed in late April or early May, and again in September; access is maintained with routine mowing of perimeters and interior paths.

Agricultural—areas leased for agricultural production with a grass buffer for public access with routine mowing of the perimeter.

Wildlife Management/Natural Areas—maintained to achieve specific vegetation and wildlife management objectives; often dependent on the establishment and maintenance of native vegetation; cut annually from January to the end of March.

egies to improve habitat and contribute to a diverse and productive landscape. They also initiated an Invasive Species Management Plan to decrease the impacts of invasive species that can severely compromise the natural landscape.

Park System Ecologist Ken Thoman also developed a Natural Resources Management Program in 1998 to be implemented throughout the parks. The program included four steps for each park: a natural resources inventory, a management plan of clearly defined goals for managing the resources, a prescription of specific actions by staff and volunteers for achieving the plan and documenting the results, and monitoring tasks for collecting feedback from staff, volunteers and visitors. Ken and other staff members continue to implement the program throughout the County parks. Staff members annually review the ongoing natural resource management in each park area in the program, including fields, forests, and aquatic areas of ponds and lakes. *(See page 62)*

To sustain New Jersey as a green and prosperous state

With development growing rapidly in the booming 1990s economy, Governor Christine Todd Whitman's Council on New Jersey Outdoors issued a report in February of 1998 recommending preserving one million of the State's two million acres of undeveloped land in the next 10 years and dedicating $200 million annually to do so.

The Council noted that, "The investment the public and private sectors make to protect open spaces is returned many times in tourism, trade, employment, and enjoyment. Since 1961, the public has voted nine times overwhelmingly to support Green Acres expenditures. This level of support means that voters clearly want to ensure that the most critical lands and waters of the State will be preserved for public and environmental benefit and not be left to the vagaries of changing real estate markets and unplanned development…To sustain New Jersey as a green and prosperous state, all levels of government as well as the nonprofit and private sectors will have to accelerate preservation efforts and double or even triple the current pace of acquisition."

Governor Whitman proposed a referendum for the November, 1998, ballot dedicating $98 million a year in sales tax revenue from 1999 to 2009 to a Garden State Preservation Trust for open space, farmland, and historic preservation and for recreational development, and dedicating $98 million a year in sales tax revenue for up to 30 years thereafter for debt service on the 1999-2009 expenditures. Voters approved the State's tenth open space referendum by a margin of almost 2 to 1.

Natural Resources Management Program - 1998

The preservation, enhancement, and stabilization of natural resources are critical to achieving the Park System's mission of providing park facilities and recreational experiences of the highest quality.

Because a diverse environment is the most stable and best able to withstand negative influences, the core objective of the Natural Resources Management Program is to maintain biological diversity: protecting the full spectrum of biological resources including the plant, animal, organic, and inorganic elements that make up the properties managed by the Park System.

Maintaining and enhancing biological diversity has numerous potential benefits: preserving examples of the natural environment of the County as land is developed; expanding the type and quality of recreational opportunities; eliminating unnecessary maintenance activities and avoiding long-term maintenance problems; generating revenue in the community by promoting outdoor recreation-related expenditures; reducing expenses for maintenance personnel, equipment, and supplies; attracting outside funding from agencies, groups, and individuals interested in natural resources.

The initial priorities of the program are to enhance tree resources and trail facilities, to manage invasive species, and to enhance resource diversity.

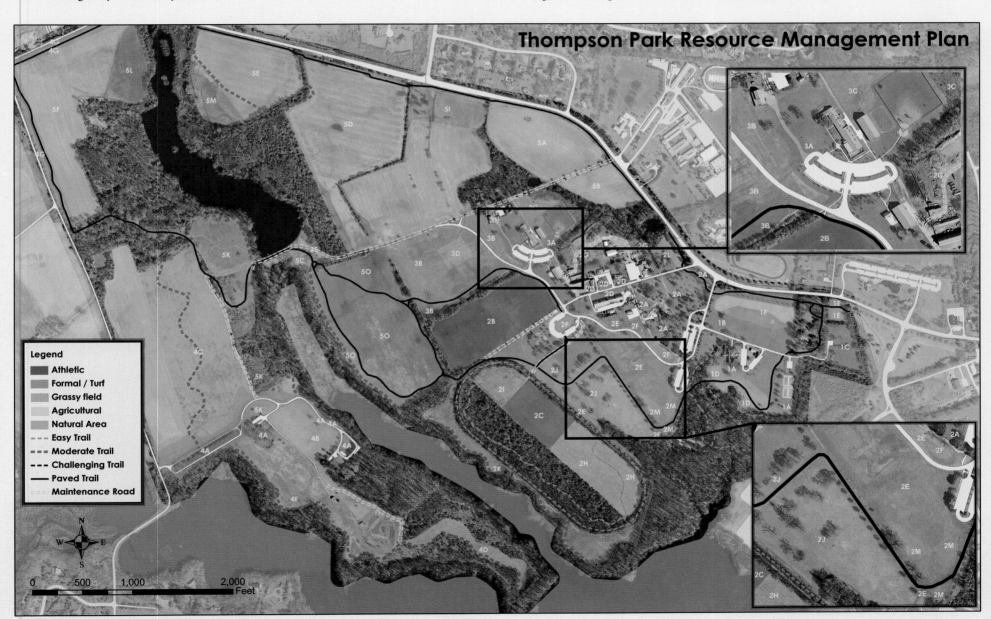

Thompson Park Resource Management Plan, 2003.

In 1999, a 416-acre tract of prime agricultural land in Holmdel that had been farmed for nearly three centuries exemplified the intense development pressure cited in the Council on New Jersey Outdoors' report. Chase Manhattan Bank owned the Holmdel site and had approval to build a one million-square-foot office campus with the potential for an additional one million square feet, but it contracted to sell the land to a developer that wanted to build 425 homes there. In a backlash against large development projects, Holmdel Township officials rezoned the land to residential use with four-acre lot minimum size, and Chase sued to block the rezoning.

When a survey showed that the majority of residents disapproved of extending sewers to the property, Holmdel officials told Chase they wouldn't approve the extension, and Chase canceled its contract with the developer. Only a coalition on an unprecedented scale in Monmouth County could raise the daunting amount of money needed to pay Chase for the high value of the land. Holmdel Township open space advocates ultimately joined forces with the Park System, the Monmouth Conservation Foundation, the Green Acres Program, and the County and State Farmland Preservation Programs to preserve the tract permanently.

The Park System added 227 acres of the Chase property to Holmdel Park, including portions of the Ramanessin-Hop Brook stream corridor, which the 1991 "Park, Recreation and Open Space Plan" had identified as a priority greenway to protect the Swimming River Reservoir water supply. The County and State preserved the two historic farms in perpetuity as farmland and sold it to two nurseries. With the addition of the former Chase lands, Holmdel Park today constitutes a greenbelt of open space extending some two and a half miles from Crawford's Corner to Middletown Road, where it joins Holmdel Township's Ramanessin Greenway.

Following up on a goal in the 1991 "Park, Recreation and Open Space Plan," the Freeholders established a regional park in Millstone Township in 1999 with the purchase of 93 acres that included Perrineville Lake, a well-known scenic landmark that was created as a mill pond in the 18th century. Perrineville Lake Park preserves rural open space and parts of Rocky Brook, a tributary of the Millstone River, which is a major source of municipal water in central New Jersey. With the assistance of Millstone Township and the Delaware and Raritan Greenway Land Trust, the Park System's continuing program of acquisitions has made Perrineville Lake Park the County's fifth largest park.

Below left: The Chase Tract in Holmdel, historically known as the Schenck Farm, in 1987.

Below right: Perrineville Lake, 1992.

THANKS to the renewal and increase of State and County funding to pursue Governor Whitman's charge to preserve open space, the Park System preserved more land through acquisitions and easements in its fifth decade than in any of its previous decades. With help from non-profits and from other government partners, the Park System preserved 5,185 acres in the 2000s despite the intense competition for land that prevailed during the decade.

The demand for trail use in Monmouth is growing

The expansion and popularity of the Park System's trails was another defining characteristic of the decade. Park System staff more than doubled the total length of trails in the parks to over 130 miles. This expansion included extending the Henry Hudson Trail, adding the Union Transportation Trail, redesigning and extending paved and unpaved trails in several parks, and creating new trails in Perrineville Lake, Turkey Swamp, Thompson, and Holmdel Parks, in Sunnyside Recreation Area, and in Hominy Hill and Charleston Springs Golf Courses. The Park System contracted for the paved trails, but staff and volunteers completed all the work on the unpaved trails.

The Henry Hudson Trail illustrated the growing popularity of trails. More than 58,000 people hiked, jogged, or bicycled its nine-mile length in 2000, and its use doubled the following year. In 1991, the "Park, Recreation and Open Space Plan" had proposed extending the trail from Aberdeen to Freehold along an unused agricultural railroad right-of-way owned by New Jersey Transit. New Jersey Transit's announcement in 2000 that it would demolish several bridges along that right-of-way precipitated County action to add it to the Henry Hudson Trail. Noting that "the demand for trail use in Monmouth is growing," the Freeholders immediately authorized the Recreation Commissioners to negotiate a lease with N.J. Transit to use the 12-mile Matawan to Freehold right-of-way for "public pedestrian and bicycle use." Park System staff subsequently secured a grant from the Federal Transportation Enhancement Program to repair and rebuild 14 bridges and to make other improvements to this southern extension of the Henry Hudson Trail, which opened in 2005.

In a 2008-2009 public interest survey, Monmouth County residents rated trails as the most popular recreation facility in the Park System.

The answer became obvious: build an arena

In the fall of 2000, the 20-year collaboration between the Park System and SPUR—Special People United to Ride—mushroomed beyond nearly everyone's expectation thanks to a remarkable fundraising event that has enormously benefited hundreds of Monmouth County children and adults with disabilities. The Therapeutic Riding program, jointly sponsored by the Park System and SPUR at Huber Woods Park, had expanded significantly since its beginnings at Thompson Park in 1981. Demand for lessons kept growing, but the outdoor facility at Huber Woods, which had to close during winter, could not serve all those who wanted to participate.

Anne Miller, a riding instructor and a former SPUR President, recalled attending her first Board Meeting in the summer of 1997, "where then-President Melissa Friedman was leading a discussion about how SPUR could provide the benefits of therapeutic riding to its students year round. The answer became obvious: build an arena. For a Board of only 20 members who were used to holding bake sales and 50/50 raffles, this was quite a task to undertake. With a 'Why not?' attitude, the group marched forward. In 1998, we hosted an Asbury Park riding event and raised over $30,000."

By 1999, when Anne was Vice President of SPUR, she mentioned to

Left: Trails like this one in Turkey Swamp Park have become the most popular recreation facilities in the Park System.

Opposite page: Manasquan Reservoir.

Tracy Boyle, a riding student of hers in Colts Neck, that SPUR needed someone to head fundraising efforts for the arena. As Tracy recalled,

I used to be deathly afraid of horses and had never been on a horse, but when I was 30, I really wanted to confront this fear. I loved horses but I was just afraid of being able to control one, the speed, and the height, all of it. A friend took me for a lesson on a wonderful older horse that just took me around and wasn't going to jump over anything, and I realized that confronting the fear was so much a self-confidence builder for me. I became impassioned by it and I wanted to learn how to jump and I wanted to own a horse.

As we were riding, she was talking about this handicapped riding facility that she was just getting involved with. In those days SPUR was open April to October. If it rained, you didn't ride. When you have a child with disabilities, what any parent will tell you is how important it is to be able to continue with something. You got so far with a child and then it was over because winter came and there was no way to continue. They could only take 30 students and they would have a wait list of up to 90 kids that wanted to participate. So we thought we would alleviate all of that when an indoor arena was built so we could serve every kid that signed up.

Tracy Boyle joined the SPUR Board and, as Anne Miller recalled, "Under the leadership of our then-President Arlene Newman, our relationship with the Park System grew even stronger and our dream of one day building an indoor arena was taking shape." By early 2000, Park System staff had developed a plan with Anne and other SPUR board members for a therapeutic riding complex with a 16,000 square foot arena and stables, outdoor riding rings, and a service area for riders and their families. Since the riding area at Huber Woods Park was too small for such a complex, Park System officials suggested locating it at the Sunnyside Recreation Area, which was designated for active recreation, easily accessible from County roads, and had large open fields.

The Park System and SPUR worked out an agreement for the Park System to build, operate, and staff the therapeutic riding complex if SPUR could raise the construction money. The Park System would cover staff and operating costs, and SPUR would provide volunteers, training, scholarships, horses, equipment, and amenities for riders and their families. The Park System design staff projected the construction cost at $850,000—a huge amount for an organization that had $15,000 in the bank and whose biggest fundraiser at the time had raised $30,000, far short of the funding needed for such an ambitious project as Sunnyside.

Jon Bon Jovi, Tracy Boyle, Patti Scialfa, and Bruce Springsteen playing at the "Off to the Races" benefit for SPUR, October 21, 2000.

TRACY BOYLE   *This room has just built a barn*

It's the invitation that comes in the mail and the way it's worded that gets people on board. The Springsteens have been part of this community for a while and I knew Patti Springsteen liked to ride, so I called her and talked to her about therapeutic riding and I asked her if she would consider being an honorary chairperson of the SPUR benefit, and she said yes. I asked Dorothea Bon Jovi to serve on the Benefit committee and she said yes, too.

I knew from past experience that if Bobby Bandiera, who's a fantastic local musician, is playing, the chances of Bruce and Jon Bon Jovi joining up and playing with him are extremely high, and Bobby agreed to play for us for next to nothing. We honored Julie Crone, the first female jockey in the Racing Hall of Fame, who used to be on the SPUR Board and was retiring from horse racing, and we produced a special video on her.

Jeannie Seuffert gave a talk—'Let me introduce you to some of my SPUR friends'—and she spoke about the kids, saying, 'The Monmouth County Park System is making this possible with your help.' She is the one responsible for everybody opening their wallet and helping because she just does such a great job getting people excited about something she believes in.

At the auction that night, there were 11 items, but they were one-of-a-kind. Bruce Springsteen donated a one-hour private guitar lesson at his home that went for $50,000. Then he auctioned off his own guitar and the whole thing just snowballed, and then the auction was over and I was able to say, 'Guess what? This room has just built a barn.' After the auction Bobby Bandiera was playing, and Bruce and Jon Bon Jovi got up and played with him for two straight hours with no break. The whole room was electrified.

I can't believe I live in a County where in one night people will come and make a powerful difference like this.

SPUR Board members launched a capital campaign in 2000 and, as Anne recalled, "Tracy took over the reins and, with incredible community support, we held a one-of-a-kind star-studded fundraiser on Saturday, October 21, at beautiful Hedgerow Stables in Middletown." SPUR's "Off to the Races" event raised $750,000—the largest amount ever raised in the County in one day. As Tracy recalled, "Jim Truncer had said he thought it was going to take several years for us to raise that kind of money. It was a fun phone call for me to make to him on that Monday morning."

What a great joint effort

Thanks to the generosity of "Off to the Races" patrons and volunteers, the Park System completed the Sunnyside Equestrian Center two years later, and SPUR and Park System staff celebrated the grand opening with three sold-out performances by Austria's famed Royal Lipizzaner Stallions. With the new arena, as SPUR President Paige Metzger wrote in the organization's spring 2003 newsletter, "We more than doubled the number of students we serve." She thanked and congratulated "those Board members, Park System staff, volunteers, and students who accomplished all this—what a great joint effort!"

Two years later, SPUR hosted a "Down the Backstretch" event in a historic Middletown barn to raise funds to help expand the Equestrian Center with offices, reception and viewing areas, and instruction and volunteer rooms. As SPUR Board member Tracy Boyle later noted, "We

have something to be so proud of. I don't think there's another park system in the country that has a handicapped riding facility, a teaching facility like this one. The school systems are calling in droves to say, 'Can we come show our kids what you do there?'" In 2009, the Equestrian Center's staff and volunteers offered 130 riding programs primarily for individuals with disabilities but also for able-bodied riders.

More recreation opportunities available to more people

At the beginning of the decade Park System staff were presenting over 3,800 programs to more than 77,000 participants annually, including more than 10,000 underserved youth in their Recreation Assistance

Below left: The Royal Lipizzaner Stallions at the Sunnyside Equestrian Center opening in 2002.

Monmouth County Park System "Recreation Services Plan," 2001

To provide year-round opportunities for persons of all ages, interests, and skills from throughout the County to engage in a variety of recreation activities, the Park System annually runs over 3,800 advertised and reserved programs in 11 categories:

Camps *for children and teens with a variety of activities from sports to crafts to nature.*

Crafts *including cooking, photography, drawing and painting, ceramics, and origami.*

Fitness and Sports *including golf, tennis, in-line skating, swimming, aerobics, tai chi, and dance.*

Gardening *encompassing planting, display, and care of indoor and outdoor plants, plus trips to gardens and flower shows.*

Historic *programs to familiarize participants with the social and cultural practices of past life in Monmouth County, plus trips to historic sites and museums.*

Nature *programs on the environment and natural history, plus trips to natural areas and natural history museums.*

Outdoor Adventures *including hiking, biking, sailing, skiing, kayaking, and horseback riding.*

Performing Arts *instruction in theatre, music and dance, plus professional performances.*

Self-improvement *programs including managing money, resume writing, and interpersonal communication.*

Travel *programs to special places and sites.*

Therapeutic *programs in multiple categories for persons with physical or mental disabilities*

To better fulfill the Visitor Services mission over the next five years:

- *Commit a percentage of each program type to Urban and Community Recreation.*
- *Distribute programs by season for year-round recreation as much as possible.*
- *Distribute programs by age group to reflect population trends and expand offerings for mixed-age and family-size audiences.*
- *Create opportunities for mainstream participation by the therapeutic population.*
- *Adjust the number and location of programs to reflect the regional distribution of population within the County.*
- *Expand program offerings on environmental issues and practices and on gardening.*
- *Expand programs for wellness and active older adults.*
- *Expand internet access to program, event and facility information, and registration.*

Program. To maximize these efforts, Superintendent of Recreation John Hoffman, Supervising Planner Faith Hahn, and other Park System staff studied population and recreation trends, community needs, and transportation issues, and they compiled their findings and recommendations in a Recreation Services Plan, which the Recreation Commissioners adopted in 2001. As John recalled, "It was a comprehensive review by the whole organization as far as the direction we would like to go with recreation in the Park System and specifically with Visitor Services programming."

Reflecting the County's growth to over 615,000 people and the diverse recreation opportunities within 36 parks spread over 12,000 acres, the Plan identified 26 actions to be implemented within 5 years. The plan, as Faith noted, focused on "making more recreation opportunities available to more people including our urban residents and people with special needs."

To increase year-round recreation opportunities for groups with special interests, including safe places for in-line skating and skateboarding, the Park System developed a Skateplex on recently-acquired land at the north end of Seven Presidents Oceanfront Park in Long Branch. The Skateplex, which opened in 2005, includes a skate park, an in-line skating rink, an open shelter, and a trail loop for skating, jogging, and walking.

Members of the Park System's Urban Recreation staff had been taking activities to urban areas for nearly 15 years. In 2003, to increase their services in Asbury Park, staff opened the Coastal Activity Center in the Salvation Army building, with regularly-scheduled art, nature, and physical recreation activities for specific age groups.

Skateplex at Seven Presidents Oceanfront Park.

Coastal Activity Center in Asbury Park.

Full utilization of its recreational potential

In the fall of 2001, the Manasquan Reservoir Environmental Center opened to the public—the culmination of several years of planning and design by Park System landscape architects and naturalists, in collaboration with consulting architects and exhibit designers. The project team, led by Supervising Landscape Architect Joe Sardonia, sited the new building on a peninsula with a spectacular view of the reservoir and focused its exhibits on wetlands ecology and wildlife and habitat protection. To orient visitors to the aquatic habitat of the area, team members created a simulated white cedar swamp and a pond at the building's entrance. They also developed hands-on exhibits on wetlands and woodlands and the ways in which people, plants, and animals use the water resources around them. The Friends of the Parks raised some of the funds for the exhibits, including a State grant and donations from corporations and individuals.

The Environmental Center's popularity with school groups and families helped raise the Manasquan Reservoir's annual visitation to over 400,000 and the Park System's overall visitation to more than four million for the first time in 2001. With its water, wildlife, nature education, and recreational opportunities, the Manasquan Reservoir became the Park System's most visited park in 2008. In 2009, it attracted more than 1.2 million people. County Planning Director Charles Pike would

certainly have been pleased to see the results of the recommendation he made in his "Recreation Study and Plan" in 1960 that "the Manasquan be developed for multiple use with full utilization of its recreational potential."

A quiet reserve

The Freeholders expanded the Board of Recreation Commissioners from seven to nine members in 2002 and asked them to develop a suitable memorial to the Monmouth County victims of the 2001 terrorist attacks. The County's September 11th Memorial Committee was chaired by architect Frank Tomaino and composed of members of victims' families and the community, Commissioners, and Park System support staff. From the time of the tragedy, people had gathered at the Mount Mitchill Scenic Overlook to view Manhattan in the distance and reflect on the losses, and the Committee selected the site for the County's 9/11 Memorial.

Monmouth County officials and Committee members dedicated the Memorial on Sunday, September 11, 2005, and unveiled its 4,500 lb. limestone eagle, poised in takeoff and clutching a beam from the World Trade Center. The Memorial honored each of the 147 Monmouth County victims with their names inscribed around the granite base of

the statue. Over 900 people visited the Overlook that day to quietly commemorate the victims. The Friends of the Parks had raised almost $300,000 for the memorial's cost, and more than 588 individuals, businesses, and organizations had contributed to their 9/11 Memorial Fund. "I have observed a quiet reserve while at the eagle that seems to be shared by all visitors," said Frank Tomaino at the dedication.

Above: Manasquan Reservoir Environmental Center.

Left: Monmouth County's 9/11 Memorial at Mount Mitchill Scenic Overlook.

Such a rewarding thing

In 2002, the Freeholders added the 125-acre Kostuk Farm to Charleston Springs Golf Course to buffer it from development and to provide trails for hiking and horseback riding. That spring, four years after the North Course opened at Charleston Springs, Dave Pease and his golf operations staff opened the South Course for limited play while the greens and fairways matured and while staff and contractors completed the 19,000-square foot Golf Center, designed by architect George Rudolph, for its May opening.

Above right: Golf Center at Charleston Springs Golf Course.

Above left: Dave Pease, the Park System's General Manager of Golf Courses at Hominy Hill Golf Course.

As Dave Pease recalled, "People were excited about Charleston Springs when we opened it, and we were excited too. Building the golf course showed what a great team we had in seeing this project through and in how we had grown and had been able to make sure we got the quality we wanted. I look at the Charleston Springs complex and it's such a rewarding thing." Joe Sardonia, who supervised the design and construction of the new golf course, was especially pleased with how the course "fits in with the landscape and reuses rain water for irrigation."

Monmouth County voters approved an increase in the County Open Space Trust funding in November, 2002, and the Freeholders announced a new Municipal Open Space Grant Program in 2003 with $2 million in annual funding from the Open Space Trust. Freeholder Director Harry Larrison and Freeholder Theodore Narozanick championed the program to enable municipalities to preserve additional open space and provide more recreational opportunities for local residents. The Program provides 50% matching grants for up to $250,000, with Urban-Aid municipalities eligible for 75% matching grants up to $250,000. The Park System administers the Program for the Freeholders, who since its inception have awarded over $12.7 million to 43 municipalities for 90 park acquisition and development projects.

The Park System received another important property donation in 2003 when Alexander J. Adair, who passed away at the age of 85, bequeathed his residence and five acres adjacent to Hartshorne Woods Park to the County. Adair was a lifelong resident of Highlands who worked for the Post Engineers at Fort Monmouth and cherished his house and wooded property on the edge of the Highlands ridge overlooking the Atlantic Ocean. Zoning regulations for the property would have permitted construction of 20 or more residential units but, after discussing preservation options with Park System and Monmouth Conservation Foundation staff members, Adair decided to donate the entire property in honor of his father, John Berry Adair, with the right to remain living there for the rest of his life. The Adair donation preserved a key buffer on the east edge of Hartshorne Woods Park.

The realization of a dream come true

In 2004, Another Park System collaboration realized its goals when the Freeholders and Recreation Commissioners joined Paul and Margo Hooker of Challenged Youth Sports to celebrate the opening of Challenger Place, a universally-accessible playground at Dorbrook Recreation Area. Mr. and Mrs. Hooker had founded Challenged Youth Sports in 1990 to provide sports programs for children with special needs. They reached out to Park System staff to work together on a barrier-free playground after receiving a letter from a 4th grader at Nut Swamp School in Middletown who wrote, "Do you know anyone who can get a playground made for disabled kids for our school? I think they should be able to play on playgrounds also. They deserve it. Just because they're disabled doesn't mean they can't have fun on playgrounds. Please help them."

Recreation Commissioner Dr. Anthony Musella, a Middletown dentist, thought that replacing the traditional playground at Dorbrook with a barrier-free playground would be a milestone in the Park System's commitment to serving youngsters with special needs. The Commissioners agreed to work with the Hookers and the non-profit Boundless Playgrounds organization from Connecticut to create Challenger Place, a play environment for all children, but with accessible features for children with disabilities.

At the Challenger Place opening, Jim Truncer credited the volunteers who spearheaded the project, "Through the tireless leadership efforts of Paul and Margo Hooker and Anthony and Mariann Musella, Challenged Youth Sports raised over $150,000 from more than 250 individuals and businesses, and this one-of-a-kind playground is now a reality." For the volunteers and for many others, as an *Asbury Park Press* reporter noted, the ribbon cutting was "the realization of a dream come true."

A month later the Park System opened its first Sprayground, just to the east of Challenger Place. Visitors splashing in and out of water-activated structures, fountains, and showers, as an *Asbury Park Press* reporter noted, quickly found it "a great place to be cool and play with water… parents and children frolicked together in the spray and sun from opening to closing." A 13-year old visitor from Rumson told the reporter, "It's pretty cool that they would build something like this. It's a great park."

A major coalition of open space advocates and agencies realized its goal in the spring of 2005 with the preservation of the 45-acre Stern Fisher property as an addition to Hartshorne Woods Park in Middletown Township. With its long frontage on Claypit Creek and magnificent view of the Navesink River, the property's high value necessitated the collaboration of multiple partners to preserve it.

Below left: Challenger Place opening at Dorbrook Recreation Area, June 2004. Tony Musella is at center, with red tie.

Below right: Sprayground at Dorbrook Recreation Area.

99-acre Timolat Farm to Huber Woods Park. The Green Acres program provided matching grants to both the County and the Foundation to support this purchase. Sloping upward from Navesink River Road, the old farm contains the McClees Creek basin with five ponds along its western boundary, and according to Foundation Trustee Larry Fink, "woods and fields that are spectacular."

At the announcement, Foundation Trustee Holly Annarella Boylan said, "instead of the 15 housing lots that it could have become, the farm will be here for our children, grandchildren, and great-grand-children." With the Stern Fisher and Timolat Farm additions to County parklands, visitors can now hike through some three and a half miles of woods and meadows from the southwestern corner of Huber Woods Park to the southeastern corner of Hartshorne Woods Park.

Keeping her legacy alive

On a cold, windy day in February, 2006, the Park System suffered a loss unprecedented in its five decades. A contractor who was improperly soldering a downspout on the Thompson Park Visitor Center, as part of the finishing touches on its renovation, sparked a fire that destroyed the building. The many staff members working in the building that morning exited safely as the fire rapidly gained intensity.

While everyone was relieved that no one had been injured, the

Above: The addition of the Stern Fisher property to Hartshorne Woods Park provides waterfront access to Claypit Creek and the Navesink River.

Right: Thompson Park Visitor Center fire, February 6, 2006.

Middletown Township contributed to the acquisition cost, and Mayor Joan A. Smith said, "We've been working closely with the County, State and the Monmouth Conservation Foundation for several years to preserve this land. Residents, including a class of fourth graders from Navesink Elementary School, had written asking us to preserve it. We are very happy to finally work out an agreement that benefits everyone. It's an incredible piece of property with scenic views and wooded spots that should and will forever belong to the public."

The Monmouth Conservation Foundation also contributed a significant amount to the project, and when the Trustees held their 28th annual dinner dance at the property later that year, President Judith Stanley Coleman told the crowd, "Preservation of Stern Fisher has been a dream for Foundation members for 15 years, and now it has finally become a reality." The County used Open Space Trust Funds and a grant from the State's Harbor and Estuary Program to complete the purchase.

The Park System and the Monmouth Conservation Foundation completed another joint acquisition effort in 2006 with the addition of the

tragedy was particularly difficult for the Visitor Center staff who had fled the fire and lost records and photographs representing decades of work and of Park System history, as well as for all those who had labored for years on the planning and execution of the building's careful renovation.

Assistant Director Bruce Gollnick summed up the loss in the May-June, 2006 issue of *Green Heritage*, "The Visitor Center had been the Park System's flagship facility for more than 38 years and represented the County's commitment to preserving the area's rich and colorful history. It's a heartbreaking loss for the Monmouth community."

Many members of the community shared personal memories of "Mrs. Thompson's house" with the Park System and expressed their desire that it should be rebuilt to look like the former mansion. Freeholder Lillian Burry felt strongly that the Park System should reconstruct the building with fire insurance proceeds, and her fellow Freeholders and the Recreation Commissioners unanimously agreed. As Gail Hunton, Park System Historic Preservation Specialist, noted in *Green Heritage*, "Recognizing the importance of Geraldine Thompson's home, where she spent so many active days in service to the community, is part of keeping her legacy alive."

With the support of the Freeholders and the community at large, Park System staff immediately began the process of reconstructing the Thompson Park Visitor Center, starting with the salvage of elements from the burned building to use in accurate replications for the new building and hiring historic architects to design the new Visitor Center in the likeness of the landmark mansion.

The improvement of our collective quality of life

After reviewing the County's open space objectives and conferring with State and municipal officials, non-profit organizations, and private citizens, a team of Park System administrators and professional staff including Faith Hahn, Andrew Coeyman, and Andy North produced a new "Monmouth County Open Space Plan" in 2006 to guide the Park System's land acquisitions over the next five years. With County parklands then totaling more than 13,000 acres, the team identified some 6,100 acres to be acquired for conservation and recreation purposes, about 10% of the 60-70,000 acres of undeveloped land in the County. As Jim Truncer noted in the Plan's Foreword,

> The landscape of Monmouth County is changing. Forests and fields are being developed. New houses and buildings replace treasured

> landmarks. Favorite woods and streams are now someone's back yard. Traffic is increasing. Sprawl is everywhere around us. While we each have a personal vision of Monmouth County in the future, I believe that we are all united in the view of a permanent landscape that includes open space for recreational pursuits, protection of water resources, preservation of natural areas, and the improvement of our collective quality of life. This is the goal of the County Open Space Plan.

The new Open Space Plan, which the County Planning Board and Recreation Commissioners adopted in August, 2006, identified five new park sites to meet future open space and recreation needs, including part of Fort Monmouth, which the U.S. Army is decommissioning, and sites in Tinton Falls, Middletown, and Marlboro. To protect water resources and to buffer existing County parkland, the Plan also recommended expanding 13 parks, including substantial additions to Perrineville Lake Park, the Yellow Brook Tract, Crosswicks Creek Greenway, Big Brook Park, Charleston Springs Golf Course, Turkey Swamp Park, and Hominy Hill Golf Course.

Once open space is gone, we can't get it back

To fulfill the land preservation goals of the Open Space Plan, the Board of Chosen Freeholders decided in the summer of 2006 to seek voter approval to convert the existing $16 million in annual open space tax revenues for the Open Space Trust Fund to a fixed rate of 1.5 cents for each $100 of equalized assessed property valuation. In announcing the referendum, Freeholder Director William C. Barham said that, "As it stands now, we are unable to acquire as much property as we would like because the cost of the land is increasing each year while our funding remains the same. Switching to a percentage rate allows us to keep pace with rising costs. This change will put us on a more solid footing for acquiring and preserving open space."

Community representatives such as Judith Stanley Coleman, President of the Monmouth Conservation Foundation, formed the Monmouth County Open Space 2006 Committee to promote passage of this key ballot question. Earlier that year, Mrs. Coleman had written to Foundation members about the urgency of action, "This is a crisis not only of open space but also of our well-being. As populations increase, preserving open space is no longer just about saving landscapes and wildlife, but about saving our quality of life, our health, and our environment from the persistent problems of land, water, and air pollution. Let's save Monmouth County before it's too late."

Monmouth County Open Space Plan Map

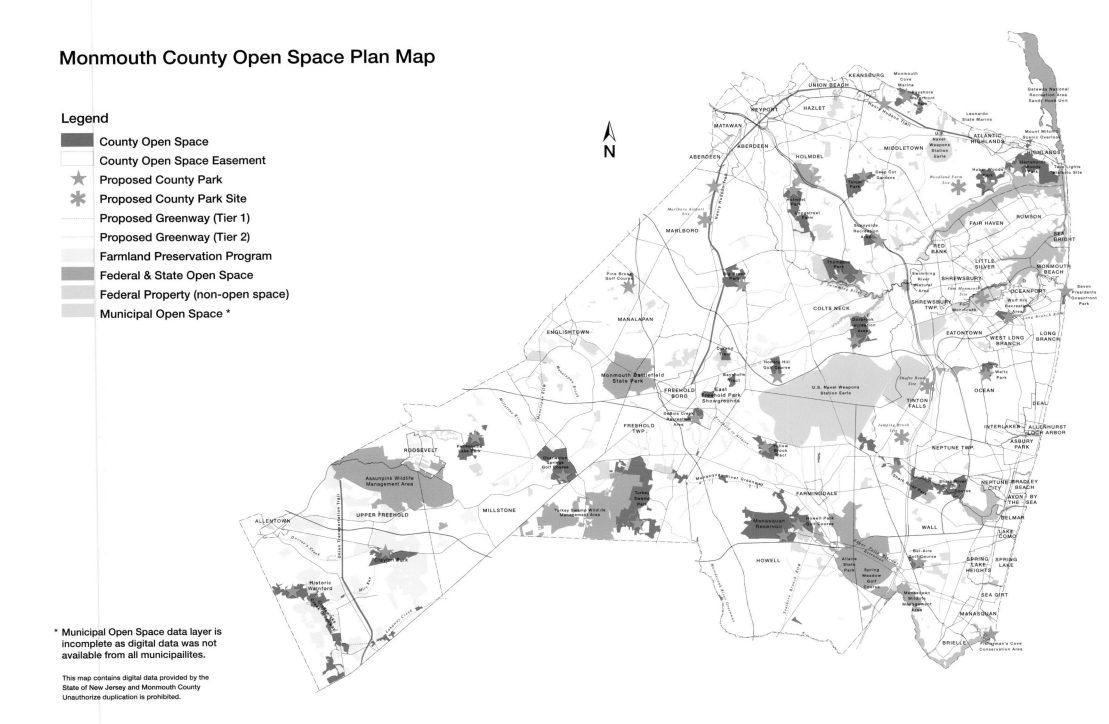

Legend

- County Open Space
- County Open Space Easement
- ★ Proposed County Park
- ✳ Proposed County Park Site
- Proposed Greenway (Tier 1)
- Proposed Greenway (Tier 2)
- Farmland Preservation Program
- Federal & State Open Space
- Federal Property (non-open space)
- Municipal Open Space *

N

* Municipal Open Space data layer is incomplete as digital data was not available from all municipailites.

This map contains digital data provided by the State of New Jersey and Monmouth County Unauthorize duplication is prohibited.

2006 Monmouth County Open Space Plan Map.

Thanks to the efforts of the Monmouth Conservation Foundation, the Open Space 2006 Committee, the Friends of the Parks, and to broad public support for open space, 65% of County voters approved the fixed-rate ballot question in the November, 2006 election, providing a strong vote of confidence for the County's program of acquiring parklands, preserving farmland and historic sites, creating recreational opportunities, and protecting water resources.

In the fall of 2006, the Monmouth Conservation Foundation celebrated its 29th anniversary with a fundraising event at the Timolat addition to Huber Woods Park, continuing its tradition of holding events at recently-preserved sites. Since 1977, the Foundation had helped preserve over 3,100 acres in Monmouth County, with more than 1,800 acres conveyed to the Park System. As Mrs. Coleman told the participants at the event, "The County needs to continue its aggressive purchase of open space. Once open space is gone, we can't get it back."

Freeholder Ted Narozanick presents a proclamation for Parks and Recreation Month to Kathleen Ragauckus and Glenn Reilly of the Park System, July 13, 1989.

Freeholder Emeritus

After serving as Freeholder for 21 years and with more than 60 years of public service, Theodore Narozanick retired at the end of 2006, and the Freeholders appropriately awarded him "Freeholder Emeritus" status, a first for the Board. Freeholder Director William Barham said, "We are all very fortunate that Ted chose to give his life and energy to Monmouth County because he improved the quality of life for everyone." From his youth in rural Englishtown, Narozanick learned the value of open space, and throughout his seven 3-year terms on the Board, he was an unswerving proponent of open space preservation and supporter of the Park System. In 1985, during his first term, Freeholder Narozanick proposed the first County Open Space tax in the state and then worked to get state enabling legislation passed after Monmouth voters had approved the referendum. In a 2004 interview, he reflected on the growth of the Park System, which he considers one of his proudest achievements.

Most people are encouraged that we've got a tremendously important parks and recreation system.

If you went out today and conducted interviews on the street, and asked people, 'What do you think of the parks, how do you like them?' they would overwhelmingly give us the top rating that they could give us. That's how much people love the parks and recreation system, and they have confidence in it and that's shown

by the attendance record. So, it's really a tremendously important aspect of County government.

I think a lot of our success has to do with the good spirit and pride of our employees. They understand what the Park System does and what it stands for. They're treated fairly, and they're respected and admired. They're really energetic and dedicated, and all of them do a great job for the Park System. Many letters come through where people have complimented our park rangers and employees for helping them in a particular problem or a situation, being very courteous and so forth, and it's great to see that type of a letter.

I'm very proud of our parks and recreation.

Inspiring us

Volunteers and visitors affirmed the popularity of County parks with significant achievements in 2007. In March of that year, Freeholder Deputy Director Lillian G. Burry presented Volunteer Service Awards recognizing extraordinary contributions to the Park System during 2006 by many generous individuals. Catherine Barry of Deal surpassed the 3,000-hour mark as a volunteer trip leader and program and office assistant, and three people contributed more than 2,000 hours of their time—Louise DelCollo of Colts Neck in Therapeutic Recreation, James Henry of Middletown at Deep Cut Gardens, and Doris Tierney of Eatontown in Outdoor Recreation.

In 2006 over 1,000 individuals volunteered in park activities ranging from summer theater to building boardwalks on trails, guiding groups of visitors at historic sites, and assisting with programs for individuals with disabilities. Freeholder Burry thanked all the volunteers for "lending the Monmouth County Park System a hand, touching our lives, and inspiring us to create a better quality of life for people of all ages and walks of life."

By June of 2007 total visitation to Monmouth County parks had passed 100 million in the 46 years since the Freeholders opened the first county park, Shark River Park, in 1961. Freeholder Burry, Recreation Commission Chairman Edward Loud, and Park System staff greeted a symbolic '100 millionth visitor' at Holmdel Park, Valerie Yannuzzi, who turned out to be a first-time visitor. Valerie, who was accompanied by her two young children, said, "Several of my friends have been raving about Holmdel Park for some time, and this was the first chance we've had to visit. The playground is terrific; it's shaded, clean, and safe. The big and small play areas make it perfect for my children." In 2007, Monmouth County Parks welcomed a record 5 million visitors.

Below left: Freeholder Director Lillian Burry and Recreation Commission Chairman Edward Loud with Volunteer Service Award winner Catherine Barry (center), March 2007.

Below right: Freeholder Director Lillian Burry and Recreation Commission Chairman Edward Loud with Valerie Yannuzzi, the Park System's '100 millionth visitor,' at Holmdel Park in June 2007.

A *unique opportunity*

In August, 2007, after many months of conferring with local, County, and State officials and reviewing proposals for future uses of the land and facilities at Fort Monmouth, Elyse LaForest, manager of the National Park Service's Federal Lands to Parks program, announced the agency's approval of the Park System's application to acquire 351 acres at Fort Monmouth. Working closely with officials from Eatontown, Oceanport, and Tinton Falls, the Park System targeted four areas within the Fort's 1,100 acres for active and passive recreation, including a youth center with gymnasium, an outdoor 25-meter swimming pool, a football complex, a bowling center, ball fields, meeting spaces, picnic areas, and a playground. The application also listed two facilities—a marina and a golf course—for conservation easements so that they would not be developed in the future for other uses. As Ms. LaForest stated in the announcement,

We have determined that the highest and best use in the public's interest of the requested parcels is for park and recreation purposes. The County's acquisition of the property will satisfy the public's need for active and passive recreational facilities in an

area of increasing population and density. The closure of Fort Monmouth presents a unique opportunity to add open space and recreational facilities in an area that is currently underserved for similar facilities and where open land does not exist.

Park System operation of these first-class facilities for public use will optimize the Army's long-term investment and continue the Fort's tradition of professional management of its recreational facilities. The Park System's stewardship of the Fort's open fields and forested wetlands will ensure permanent protection of these natural resources. The Fort Monmouth Final Reuse and Redevelopment Plan, adopted in September, 2008, is largely consistent with the Park System's application. Federal action on the Plan, including transfer of Fort Monmouth property to the County, is pending. Fort Monmouth is currently slated for closing in 2011.

New Jersey and Monmouth County voters approved the State's twelfth open space bond act in 2007, dedicating $200 million for the Garden State Preservation Trust to preserve open space, farmland, and historic buildings. The 2006 "Monmouth County Open Space Plan" provided the acquisitions staff with a number of properties that might be suitable for potential Green Acres funding from this bond act.

In October, 2008, Monmouth County lost one of its most ardent proponents of county history and parks when Daniel Ward Seitz died at the age of 77. Seitz was a direct descendant of Richard Hartshorne, one of the first Europeans to settle in the region during the late 1600s, and a long-time resident of Portland Place, his family's ancestral home in the Locust section of Middletown.

A founding member of the Hartshorne Woods Association, which had advocated preservation of the woods as county parkland since the 1960s, Seitz was also a trustee of the Monmouth County Historical Association for more than 40 years. He took great pride in being one of the first members of the Friends of the Parks, serving on the Board from 1992 until his death and as Friends President from 1993 to 1995.

In the ultimate demonstration of his commitment to preserving land and historic sites, Seitz donated Portland Place and its 4.7 acres to the Park System, writing in his will, "This historic property known as Portland Place, which it has been my good fortune to enjoy, will be used for educational, conservation, and museum purposes only by the Monmouth County Park System as a complement to Hartshorne Woods Park...in honor of the values which Richard Hartshorne, the first of the family to come to America and to build on this land, exemplified by his actions in public service."

Dan Seitz at Portland Place in 2006.

Strive to stay ahead

To help the Park System gauge the needs and interests of the public it serves, the Recreation Commissioners contracted with a nationally-recognized survey research firm to conduct the "Monmouth County Citizen Opinion and Interest Survey" over the winter of 2008-2009. Survey participants identified the 'preservation of open space and the environment' and the 'protection of forested areas from development' as the two top benefits that parks provide, and more than 90% favored the 'continued acquisition of open space.' Respondents also indicated that they used County parks for indoor and outdoor recreation more than any other public or private facilities, with 91% of them having visited County Parks within 12 months of the survey date.

Trails and playgrounds ranked as the most popular facilities, and 51% of those surveyed rated the condition of County parks as 'excellent,' compared to a national average of 30%, while 46% rated the condition of County parks as 'good.' The survey results indicated that the Park System needs to improve the rate of program participation, increase brand recognition, and educate the public about how parks and recreation promote good health and physical fitness. The Park System received the highest rating for customer satisfaction ever recorded by the research firm, with 45% of participants describing themselves as 'very satisfied' with the overall value they received, nearly double the national average of 24%.

In March, 2009, the Park System received its fourth 5-year accreditation from CAPRA—the Commission for Accreditation of Park and Recreation Agencies, which noted in its report,

The Park System is rich with institutional knowledge and, despite the longevity of employees, the agency has continued to strive to stay ahead of trends and best practices. Their focus on natural resources coupled with the strength of the Friends groups and citizen support have allowed the agency to preserve open space and educate the public about the value of parks and recreation. The Acquisition and Design Division has an exceptional process of planning for continuing open space acquisition plus a comprehensive design program for capital repair and improvement to agency facilities.

Having a personnel director on staff and having detailed procedures for personnel management is another strength of the agency. Orienting new personnel and providing employee housing are beneficial to the agency and employees. The inventory and diversity of facilities and organization of maintenance department and the agency's internal budgeting and development process are comprehensive and forward thinking. Administrative space is both functional and contributory towards the mission of the agency.

Proudly resumes its place

On a perfect summer day in July, 2009, County officials and Park System staff welcomed almost 400 people who came to celebrate the dedication of the new Thompson Park Visitor Center. As the *Asbury Park Press* noted, "Geraldine Thompson certainly would have approved," of the Park System's on-schedule and on-budget reconstruction of her 1896 mansion that burned to the ground in 2006. Rebuilt entirely with the County's insurance claim settlement, the new Visitor Center replicates many of the original historic features, with some expanded public rooms and full accessibility. Freeholder Lillian Burry told the assembled guests, "The new Visitor Center respects the historic

character of the former building and honors Geraldine Thompson's legacy to the people of Monmouth County. Today, three years after the fire, this mansion proudly resumes its place as the 'crown jewel' of the County Park System."

County and Park officials and many County residents gathered in November, 2009, to dedicate Tony's Place, a nearly one-third acre playground at Seven Presidents Oceanfront Park in Long Branch that includes special adaptive equipment for children with disabilities. As they had done five years earlier for Challenger Place at Dorbrook Recreation Area, Paul and Margo Hooker raised approximately $140,000 through their non-profit Challenged Youth Sports to help pay for this playground. Park System officials located the playground, which staff landscape architect Richard Pillar designed, at Seven Presidents because of its high visitation and urban location. The Recreation Commissioners named the new playground in honor of the late Dr. Anthony "Tony" Musella, one of their former members who championed recreation opportunities for children with special needs.

As Freeholder Director Barbara J. McMorrow said at the dedication, "The Park System works to provide us with safe, clean, and environmentally friendly places to recreate, but this particular playground is even more meaningful because it is named for someone who cared about and understood the needs of individuals with disabilities. Tony Musella left a legacy that we are very proud to honor and carry forward." Dr. Musella had served as a Recreation Commissioner for 13 years, including a term as vice chairman, before his premature death in 2006. His wife, Mariann Musella, said that, "Tony would have been quite pleased that another playground has been created for all the children in our county."

Despite the economic downturn in 2009, voters in Monmouth County and New Jersey approved the Garden State Preservation Trust Bond Act, the State's thirteenth open space referendum, for $400 million. Since the first Green Acres Bond Act of 1961, State and County voters have approved nearly $3.4 billion of grants and low interest loans for State, county, and municipal preservation of open space, farmland, flood zones, and historic sites. In its first five decades, the Park System received from these bond acts $31.3 million in grants and $26.5 million in loans for land acquisition, plus $1.2 million for park development projects, for a total of $59 million. The Park System was awarded $2.4 million in historic preservation grants from several of the bond acts for three of its historic sites.

The Monmouth Conservation Foundation, other land preservation groups, and many municipalities in the County have received millions of dollars in grants from the 13 bond acts. With the hundreds of thousands of acres and the many historic sites preserved throughout the State, it is no wonder that Green Acres is widely recognized as the most successful public open space preservation program in the United States, and future generations will increasingly value this impressive legacy.

By the end of its first 50 years in 2009, the Park System had preserved 14,646 acres within County parks, plus another 1,987 acres through easements, for a total of 16,633 acres of preserved open space. The Park System offered 4,235 recreational and cultural programs in 2009, and program attendance reached 99,733. Annual visitation at County Parks climbed 3% in 2009 to reach its highest level ever—5,282,469 visitors. Nearly 900 volunteers working in 1,315 positions contributed 21,003 hours of their time in 2009 to enhancing the Park System and the experience of its visitors. Another 54 volunteers contributed 458 hours to helping the Friends of the Parks raise funds and undertake projects to improve the Park System.

Since its creation, the Park System has benefited not only from donations of time and talent but also from transfers and gifts of land as well as other personal property. The value of donations in 2009 totaled more than $7 million. To date, the total value of donations received in support of the Park System, based upon the value as of the date of donation, has exceeded $38 million.

Park System revenue surpassed $14 million in 2009, with over $9 million coming from the County's six golf courses and $1.9 million from recreational programs and activities. The Park System is exploring innovative ways to increase this revenue, which sustains basic operations and reduces dependence on general County tax revenues. The dual task of providing quality programs and activities, while at the same time generating revenue to help support the Park System's overall budget, reflects the need for government agencies to be more entrepreneurial as municipal, County, and State budgets are all under stress. Through the continued support of the Freeholders and the citizens of Monmouth County, and with the development of various sources of revenue, the Park System will continue to provide Monmouth County residents with quality facilities and services and free access to their County park lands.

Above: Thompson Park Visitor Center opening, July 12, 2009.

Left: Thompson Park Day.

Below: Holmdel Park.

Opposite page: Tatum Park.

The next fifty years

Joseph Irwin, Charles Pike, and all the other County leaders who 50 years ago envisioned a system of open space and recreation in Monmouth County would be gratified to see today what their vision inspired. The outstanding natural, historical, and recreational resources that now comprise the Park System are their legacy and the legacy of all the donors, citizens, officials, staff, volunteers, and partners who have contributed to building what many people consider to be one of the finest county park systems in the United States.

In contemplating the next 50 years of providing open space and recreation, the people of Monmouth County must remain committed to a strong system of County parks to preserve and protect their rich natural environment and cultural resources and to provide superior recreation facilities for all residents. Continued sound fiscal management, ongoing investment, strong professional leadership, and active public support will all be necessary to build on the Park System's exceptional record of preservation, stewardship, and service.

Preservation

The need to preserve critical and special open spaces in Monmouth County will continue as increases in population and density place more stress on our natural resources and generate more demand for recreation. With technological progress, more and more people will be working, shopping, learning, and interacting with each other from homes, and they will increasingly seek open space and recreation to balance their lives.

Preservation priorities will continue to include: greenways along the County's major stream corridors to protect water supply and habitat for plants and wildlife; special natural resources of fields and forests, water and wetlands, marshes and coastlines to preserve the local and regional ecology; open spaces adjacent to existing parks to protect them from encroachments; and linkages connecting parks and communities.

Smart preservation strategies that pool talent and resources from governments, non-profits, and private citizens will become ever more important as growing demands for all kinds of services place increasing burdens on public resources.

Among the preservation opportunities on the horizon, the acquisition of surplus property at Fort Monmouth following its scheduled closing in 2011 holds great promise to convert quality military recreation facilities to public use, create new year-round facilities, and preserve natural areas in the populated Coastal Region of the County, which will continue to grow in density. The anticipated transfer of land from Fort Monmouth to the Park System will follow the precedent of similar transfers of former military sites that are now key components of Hartshorne Woods, Holmdel, and Tatum Parks.

Stewardship

The Park System's stewardship of the lands it holds and manages for the public will become increasingly valuable as parks gradually become islands of public open space within denser land uses. Staff

initiatives in ecological management will need to grow significantly as science, technology, and collaborations expand the possibilities for conserving natural resources.

The Park System's stewardship of historic resources will also gain importance as more and more historic sites succumb to modern development. While careful and authentic preservation of the physical fabric of the County's historic sites must continue to be a priority, the importance of interpreting their meaning to the public will increase as fewer and fewer sites remain to convey the County's rich heritage to future generations.

The stewardship of infrastructure and facilities with a commitment to quality must continue to be a hallmark of Monmouth County parks and will be enhanced by technological and managerial innovations.

Service

The Park System's commitment to provide diverse recreational opportunities for people of all ages and of varying abilities will need to capitalize on innovative ways to use facilities, technologies, and human resources. Recreational programs and activities must continue to evolve to meet the changing needs and demands of an increasingly diverse and dense population.

Linkages and transportation between parks and communities will become increasingly important to maximize public and private investment in the parks and to serve a growing population.

The Park System's entrepreneurial focus on collaborations and on raising revenue from users to help support operations will grow as the need to maximize the use of public funds increases over time.

Park System staff, both behind the scenes and on the front line, have enhanced the organization's reputation by their professionalism and pleasant interaction with visitors. This tradition will continue to grow as employees embrace their work of being stewards of natural and historic places and sharing them with the public in meaningful ways.

Service is a fitting note on which to conclude this history of the Monmouth County Park System's first 50 years. The System's founders and all the people who have built it, donated their assets and time to it, and have operated it over the last five decades have all shared a common goal—to serve the public in Monmouth County with the best open space and recreation experiences possible. Their legacy is visible throughout the County, and future generations will cherish and expand it.

The County Parks In 2009: Acreage By Category

Open Lands
Baysholm Tract..71
Yellow Brook Tract.....................................338

Recreation Areas
DeBois Creek Recreation Area 165
Dorbrook Recreation Area 535
Sunnyside Recreation Area 135
Wolf Hill Recreation Area 92

Regional Parks
Bayshore Waterfront Park 227
Big Brook Park..379
Clayton Park...437
Hartshorne Woods Park.............................793
Holmdel Park..565
Huber Woods Park......................................376
Perrineville Lake Park 928
Shark River Park...957
Tatum Park..366
Thompson Park...667
Turkey Swamp Park.................................2,143

Special Use Areas
Deep Cut Gardens 54
East Freehold Showgrounds.........................81
Historic Longstreet Farm...............................9
Historic Walnford 36
Manasquan Reservoir 1,204
Monmouth Cove Marina..............................11
Mount Mitchill Scenic Overlook.................12
Seven Presidents Oceanfront Park...............38

Unclassified
Durand Tract (leased to Freehold Twp.).......94
Weltz Park..165

Conservation Area
Fisherman's Cove...55

Golf Courses
Bel-Aire 114
Charleston Springs.....................................781
Hominy Hill...262
Howell Park..311
Pine Brook..61
Shark River...176

Greenways
Crosswicks Creek 1,444
Henry Hudson Trail 100
Manasquan River..337
Metedeconk River 121
Union Transportation Trail.............................6

**Total acres owned and/or managed
by the Park System 14,646***

EASEMENTS 1,987

TOTAL ACRES PRESERVED 16,633

**This number includes 1,135 park acres under the following
Use Agreements: 1,052 acres at the Manasquan Reservoir
owned by the NJ Water Supply Authority and leased to the
Park System for perpetual use; 83 acres of the Henry Hudson
Trail are county-owned and managed by Park System.*

Part II: Monmouth County Parks

1. Shark River Park | 1960–24 ACRES; 2009–957 ACRES

THIS FIRST Monmouth County park originated when the N.J. Highway Authority completed the Garden State Parkway and declared 24 acres of adjacent land as surplus. The land included part of a former Girl Scout camp, fields, and forested wetlands along the Shark River. With its potential for both recreation and protection of a stream corridor, and its proximity to populated shore towns, County leaders considered it ideal for their first regional park, and they bought it in 1960.

In developing Shark River Park, County leaders established two precedents for their future parks—serving visitors of all age groups year round with multiple recreation opportunities and leveraging the County's investment with other resources. Their plan included trails

along the river, a four-acre pond for fishing and skating, picnic tables and grills, playing fields, a playground, parking, restrooms, and a shelter building, and they enlisted the State's Soil Conservation Service to dig the pond and arranged for prisoners to help with the construction. County leaders opened the park in 1961 and its immediate popularity led Neptune Township officials to donate 40 acres of adjacent wetlands and woods to expand the park.

In the ensuing five decades, the Park System has expanded Shark River Park eastward along both sides of the river, protecting the Shark River watershed with additional woods, fields, and wetlands to encompass 957 acres, nearly 40 times its original size. It is the now the County's second largest regional park and has nine miles of multi-use trails for hiking, running, biking, and horseback riding.

The park is located on New Jersey's outer coastal plain where the terrain is generally flat, the soils are sandy remnants of the ancient seabed, and the vegetation represents the northern edge of the New Jersey Pine Barrens, an internationally recognized landscape. It is a linear park along both sides of the Shark River, with its eastern border near the Shark River Basin. The Park and the County's adjacent Shark River Golf Course protect about 16% of the Shark River watershed.

Most of the park is forested and almost half is lowlands. The forest community is typical of the Pine Barrens, with pitch pine dominating, and including red maple and various oak species. Huckleberries and blueberries provide a low sparse understory in the higher and drier areas, and swamp azalea and southern magnolia grow in lower and wetter areas. Cranberries and sundews thrive in sandy areas with a shallow water table, and Atlantic white cedar woodlands and sphagnum moss hummocks thrive in the saturated lowlands. The core of the forest is relatively undisturbed by invasive species. Three notable plant species of local abundance are clubmoss, pink lady's slipper, and a rare occurrence of American climbing fern in specific locales.

Wildlife within Shark River Park includes bald eagles, barn and great horned owls, cormorants, great blue and green herons, ospreys, red bats, scarlet tanagers, wood ducks, wild turkeys, coyotes, red foxes, box and snapping turtles, black racer snakes, and largemouth bass.

2. Holmdel Park | 1962–41 ACRES; 2009–574 ACRES

WITH its prime location and multiple attractions, Holmdel Park was the County's most visited park for four decades and it now competes with the Manasquan Reservoir for that annual distinction. County officials established Holmdel Park in 1962 by securing the first Green Acres matching grant in the State to purchase 41 acres of prime farmland from William and Mary J. Riker. The County used Green Acres matching grants to purchase 131 acres of the adjacent Longstreet Farm from William and Mary Holmes Duncan in 1963, and six acres with the historic Longstreet farmstead in 1967.

The Park System created hiking trails through the forested portion of the new park, converted the old apple orchard to a sledding hill, and the old farm fields to playfields, open lawn, and a picnic area. The State's Soil Conservation Service designed a six-acre pond for fishing and skating and County prisoners provided some of the general labor for park improvements.

The Monmouth County Shade Tree Commission started a 22-acre arboretum at the south end of the park in 1963 and arranged for Robert B. Clark, the Senior Curator if the L.H. Bailey Hortorium at Cornell University, to draw up the plans for it. Commission chairman William Duryea and other members arranged for local nurseries to donate 87 specimen trees, including crabapples, cherries, and hollies. Since then the Commission has expanded the arboretum to more than 3,000 trees and shrubs, and recently named it the David C. Shaw Arboretum in honor of the superintendent who oversaw it from 1963 to 2002.

When County officials learned in 1963 that the U.S. Army was going to phase out its 18-acre Cold War Nike Missile Battery on the hill north of the Park, they immediately requested the land to add it to the Park. The Federal Government transferred the surplus property in 1972, and the Park System installed tennis courts, a picnic area, and a fitness course where the old facilities had been, and created trails in the remaining natural areas.

After a multi-year effort, a coalition involving Monmouth County, Holmdel Township, the Monmouth Conservation Foundation, and the Green Acres program in 2001 preserved the "Chase Tract"—416 acres of prime farmland formerly slated for development southwest of Holmdel Park. The Park System added 227 acres of this land, some of which had once been part of Longstreet Farm, to Holmdel Park as a natural area with fields and trails along the Ramanessin Brook.

Longstreet Farm

THE LONGSTREET FARM homestead is one of the best preserved historic farmsteads in New Jersey and one of the Park System's most popular sites, attracting over 100,000 visitors a year to see how farm families lived in the 1890s. When English and Dutch immigrants established Middletown around 1680, the Longstreet Farm land was part of an 1,800-acre plantation settled by Richard Stout, an Englishman, and Penelope Van Princis Stout, his Dutch wife.

The central portion of the Longstreet House is the oldest existing structure on the farm, and was built as a one-and-one-half story Dutch-American House in the mid to late 18th century, probably by Hendrick and Lydia Hendrickson. Their daughter, Williampe, married Aaron Longstreet in 1778, and they built the two-story section before 1798, when the Federal Direct Tax assessment for Middletown Township recorded its dimensions and number of windows. They also built the massive Dutch Barn, which the Park System dated through dendrochronology to 1792. The farm passed down through five generations to Mary Longstreet Holmes, who was born on the farm in 1901 and lived there her entire life. She and her husband, William Duncan, sold the farm to the County. Mary Holmes Duncan lived there until her death in 1977.

Park System staff decided to interpret Longstreet Farm to the 1890s, which older members of the County's Agricultural Committee remembered as a period of major transition as farmers switched from horses to tractors. Tom Kellers, who was in charge of the interpretation in the 1970s, recently recalled that, "barn doors opened up all over the county" and farmers dropped off tools and equipment they had been saving for decades. The staff opened the Longstreet barn complex in 1971 with farm animals and costumed interpreters, and it quickly became a popular attraction for families and school groups. The Park System subsequently restored the Longstreet House to the 1890s and opened it in 1983. As farming has continued to disappear, Longstreet Farm provides children and adult visitors with an increasingly valuable glimpse into the way people lived off the land in Monmouth County's agricultural past.

Holmdel Park is on the cuesta or gently-sloping ridge that runs from Hartshorne Woods Park in the northeast corner of the County to the Clayton Park area in the southwest. It has the largest height variation of all the County Parks—from 300 feet above sea level in the Hilltop area, to 70 feet above sea level at the lowest point on the Ramanessin Brook. The park contains the headwaters of the Ramanessin Brook, which drains to the Swimming River Reservoir.

About two-thirds of the park is forested, with fields and a six-acre pond on the other third. The old growth upland forest is dominated by American beech, northern red oak. and tulip poplar trees, and has a sparse understory of American hornbeam trees, maple-leaf and arrowwood viburnam shrubs, and Canada mayflower perennials. Low-lying forested areas are dominated by red maple and green ash trees, with an understory of spicebush, and skunk-cabbage in the more saturated wetlands. The Ramanessin section contains some rare strawberry bush despite the prevalence of deer. Some notable herbaceous plants include foamflower, a rare New Jersey Species, and notable spring ephemerals along the Marsh

Trail: early meadow rue, round-leaved wintergreen, and round-lobed hepatica.

Most of the 182 acres of fields in the park are meadows with warm-season native grasses and plants like Goldenrod that provide pleasant vistas and habitat for field-nesting birds and insects. Some of the remaining fields with cool-season grasses are maintained as 'hay fields,' with infrequent mowing. The two man-made ponds contain stocked trout, and their shorelines have been planted with native vegetation to provide habitats for butterflies and aquatic insects. Notable wildlife sightings in the park include pileated woodpeckers, great-horned owls, painted turtles, and ring-necked ducks.

3. Turkey Swamp Park | 1963–272 ACRES; 2009–2,142 ACRES

TURKEY SWAMP PARK is the County's largest park and together with the adjacent State-owned 2,455-acre Turkey Swamp Wildlife Management Area preserves nearly 4,600 acres, the vast majority in their natural condition, on the northern fringe of the Pine Barrens. The relatively flat area got its name from the prevalence of wild turkeys and from the high water table that creates swampy conditions in low areas. Native Americans occupied the area because of its abundant wildlife, and European Americans later farmed some of the higher, tillable areas with moderate results.

County officials used Green Acres matching grants to establish this regional park in 1963 with the purchase of the 189-acre Bohnke Farm and the adjacent 83-acre Schnitzler property on Georgia Tavern Road. The Park System created hiking trails and camping and picnicking areas, and used a Federal Land and Water Conservation Fund grant to create a 17-acre lake for boating and fishing. In a 1978 excavation, archaeologists unearthed Native American artifacts in the Park (pictured right).

In 1993, the County acquired the adjacent 303-acre Nomoco Camp from the Monmouth Council of Girl Scouts to expand the Park with group camping opportunities.

More than 90% of the current acreage in the Park is forested, and a little over half is wetland that includes the headwaters of the Manasquan River, the water source for much of southeastern Monmouth, and the Metedeconk River, which drains to the Barnegat Bay. The dominant trees

in the Park are red maple, sweet and black gum, shortleaf and pitch pines, and nine species of oaks. Shrubs include sweet pepperbush, blue huckleberry, swamp sweetbells, greenbriar, and blueberry. Two notable perennials in the Park are the crane-fly orchid, which has leaves in the winter and flowers in the summer, and foxtail clubmoss. Eastern red cedars have grown up on the former farm fields along with native grasses. The woods turn brilliant red in the fall when blueberries and sweet and black gum change color. Resource management efforts in the Park include treating for the exotic gypsy moth caterpillars that each year emerge and eat the oak trees clean of all leaves.

The Park and the State's adjacent Turkey Swamp Wildlife Management Area, which includes nearly 4,000 acres of public and private land, provide a large contiguous habitat for larger wildlife like coyote and barred, screech and great horned owls, for forest nesting birds like hermit thrush, eastern phoebe, scarlet tanager, and golden-crowned kinglet, and for brown bats and an increasing population of wild turkey. The lake hosts visiting spotted and solitary sandpipers, woodcock, pied-billed grebe, hooded merganser, cormorant, egrets, heron, and belted kingfisher. An unusual species along the Park's Metedeconk Trail is the Allegheny mound ant, which builds 5' wide by 2.5' tall mounds in the driest areas so they won't get flooded in the wet season.

WITH its rustic wooded setting and challenging fairways, Howell Park Golf Course often seems to the golfers who play there that it must have started as a private club, but the Park System built the course on the site of a former farm 40 years ago to meet the growing demand for golf. Eatontown realtor and golf enthusiast Harold Lindemann thought that the gently rolling fields, good soils, and ponds of the 302-acre Windsor Stock Farm, an old dairy farm in Howell Township, would make a fine golf course, and he recommended to the Freeholders that they purchase the property from the Estate of Carl F. Gamer.

The Park System commissioned the noted golf course architect Francis Duane to design the course to be aesthetically pleasing as well as challenging. Duane earned a degree in landscape architecture from Syracuse University and had worked with the famed golf course architect Robert Trent Jones for several years before starting his own firm. He designed several public and private courses in Bergen County, on Long Island and in upstate New York, and he later collaborated with Arnold Palmer on golf courses in South Carolina, California, and Hawaii. For Howell Park, Duane designed an 18-hole, par 72 golf course with 6,964 yards of play.

According to Dave Pease, the Park System's General Manager of Golf Courses who began working at the Park System in 1977, the Francis Duane design at Howell "is second to none with regard to the challenge of the game in a parkland design. The routing of the course, and the shot making battles that were placed in the design, are extremely challenging and right on the top of the game. The strength of the course and the concepts that were put into it are very unique, and that's probably why it has been ranked so high in the public golf courses in the country, because of its playability as well as the strength of its design." Howell Park Golf Course consistently ranks among the top 50 public golf courses in the country.

In developing the golf course, the Park System preserved about 40% of the park land as forest to help protect the Manasquan River watershed. The river runs along the northeast border of the Park, and beautiful wildflowers bloom along its banks in the spring. The Timber Swamp Brook bisects the course with a pond close to the center of the Park and drains to the Manasquan. The forest contains a variety of trees: sweet and black gum, black walnut, red maple, black cherry, tulip poplar, pitch pine, and red and chestnut oaks. Native shrubs in the Park include sweet pepperbush, mapleleaf and arrowwood viburnum, blue huckleberry, and serviceberry. Interesting perennials include smooth Solomon's seal and strawberry bush.

The popular Manasquan River Canoe Race, which the Park System first sponsored in 1970, annually draws many participants to the canoe launching area in the park.

5. Thompson Park | 1968–215 ACRES; 2009–667 ACRES

GERALDINE LIVINGSTON THOMPSON donated 215 acres of Brookdale Farm, one of New Jersey's premier thoroughbred horse estates, to Monmouth County when she died in 1967 at the age of 95. She first mentioned that she might donate her land for a County park and a wildlife sanctuary in 1957, and later told a reporter, "We've got to live with nature. The children have to feel the ground beneath them and go out in the woods and see the trees and birds."

Mrs. Thompson's generous donation included an impressive complex of buildings representing the multiple owners of the land over three centuries. The oldest house on the property, built by Thomas Lloyd in 1786, was the largest house in Middletown Township recorded in the 1798 Federal Direct Tax assessment. David Dunham Withers bought the Lloyd farm in 1872 and established the Brookdale Breeding and Stock Farm there, eventually expanding it to 838 acres that became known as the Brookdale Triangle. Withers had amassed a cotton fortune in New Orleans, and after the Civil War he returned to New York to pursue his interests in shipping and horse racing. Withers became a thoroughbred racing authority, and he bought Monmouth Park with some other breeders in 1878 and made it one of the country's pre-eminent race tracks. He employed over 100 people at Brookdale Farm, where he built a house for himself, a 300-ft. long training barn, and other barns for his 90 horses, and two race tracks.

William P. Thompson, who had served as a colonel in the Confederate Army and was president of the National Lead Company and a former vice-president of the Standard Oil Company, purchased Brookdale Farm in 1893 and commissioned the noted New York architects Carrere and Hastings, designers of the New York Public Library, to expand Withers' house into a Georgian Revival mansion. Thompson was also an authority on horse racing and bred and trained nearly 200 race horses, including many famous ones, at Brookdale Farm. When he died unexpectedly in 1896, his son Lewis Steenrod Thompson completed the house and married Geraldine Livingston Morgan that same year (mansion, stable hands and 40-stall training barn pictured left in 1906).

Geraldine grew up near Hyde Park, New York, where she became friends with Franklin D. Roosevelt and his cousin Eleanor Roosevelt, and Geraldine entertained Mrs. Roosevelt at Brookdale Farm on several occasions. Mrs. Thompson was politically active and in 1923 she became the first female New Jersey delegate to a Republican National Convention. In 1931 she was the first woman to receive an honorary Master of Philosophy degree from Rutgers University. Her support of prison reform, education, public health, and land conservation, including preserving Island Beach as a state park, brought her numerous honors and led many people to call her the "First Lady of Monmouth County" and "New Jersey's First Lady."

In 1985, the County more than tripled the size of Thompson Park with the acquisition of the 334-acre Marlu Farm, which had once been a part of Brookdale Farm, and the adjacent 118-acre Cheeca Farm to preserve the land from being developed and to protect the Swimming River Reservoir. Today, Thompson Park and Holmdel Township's 83-acre Cross Farm Park on the east side of Longbridge Road protect nearly two miles of shoreline on the north side of the Swimming River Reservoir.

Brookdale Farm was for many decades the showplace of Monmouth County's horse farm estates, and today Thompson Park is the Park System's headquarters and crown jewel. With 14 miles of trails, soccer and rugby fields, tennis courts, a playground, a fishing lake, an off-leash dog area, the Creative Arts Center, and its many programs and activities, Thompson Park attracted the fourth highest visitation in the Park System in 2009.

Reflecting the use of the landscape over three centuries, Thompson Park today is a mosaic of lawns, specimen estate trees, playing fields, agricultural fields, hedgerows, shrublands, and woods. Almost 75% of the land is open, with about one-third of it maintained as natural areas, with cool-season grassy fields resembling hayfields and old fields dominated by a variety of warm-season native grasses like broomsedge and little bluestem and other more colorful native perennials like goldenrod. All these grassy fields provide a pastoral contrast to the formal lawns and grounds of the old estate and the park facilities. About one-quarter of the open areas are agricultural fields leased to farmers, another quarter are open play fields, and about 10% are formal athletic fields. Park ecologists are managing several ongoing restoration projects to remove invasive species, promote reforestation, and nurture old fields and mature woodlands in the Park.

Geraldine Thompson wanted her land to be a sanctuary for birds, and she would be pleased to see the many species of birds in the Park today. The grassy fields provide habitat for flying insect feeders like eastern bluebirds and purple martins and for field-dependent birds like harriers, meadowlarks, and sparrows. Other notable field birds in the Park include cedar waxwing, eastern kingbird, indigo bunting, sand hill crane, sharp-shinned hawk, and Coopers hawk. Hedgerows and estate and farm trees around the Park provide foraging and resting areas for many birds, especially during migration periods, including some occasional or rare species like northern shrike, yellow-billed cuckoo, and blue grosbeak.

The wooded 25% of the Park includes remnants of old growth forest, which has remained forest for at least 150 years, with stands of American beech and red, white and black oak, and an understory of maple-leaf viburnum and in some areas mountain laurel. The 10-acre forest on the Cheeca Farm includes shagbark hickory and American elm, and a great horned owl pair often utilize these woods for breeding. A large area of trout lily wildflowers provides an attractive spring display in the woods along the reservoir. The forested areas and grounds also host screech owl, common redpoll, great horned owl, hooded warbler, orchard oriole, pine warbler, and foraging bald eagle, and wetland areas host clapper rail, glossy ibis, lesser yellowlegs, and greater yellowlegs.

The expansion of the Swimming River Reservoir in the 1960s and the formation of the 22-acre Marlu Lake from the flooding of Borden's Brook have created some significant water habitat for notable species like the American bittern, a bird of the heron family that wades along the forested shorelines, and bald eagles that nest and forage in the vicinity.

6. Baysholm Tract | 1969–35 ACRES; 2009–71 ACRES

GERALDINE THOMPSON'S donation of Brookdale Farm to the Park System in 1967 may have inspired Helen Hermann of West Long Branch to donate Baysholm, her farm in northwest Freehold Township. Miss Hermann was born in 1902 in Manhattan and grew up spending summers with her family in the Elberon section of Long Branch, where she became an avid tennis player. She attended Bryn Mawr College, where she excelled in math, earned a master's degree at Columbia University, and later worked for Franklin Delano Roosevelt. She never married but volunteered for many years to help children, and she co-founded the Children's Psychiatric Center, which is now CPC Behavioral Healthcare in Eatontown. She left half of her substantial estate to the organization, which named its Helen Hermann Counseling Center in Red Bank and its annual Helen Hermann Community Service Award in her honor.

In 1946, Miss Hermann (pictured right) bought the 71-acre William Wikoff Farm in Freehold Township and named it Baysholm from an Old English word for 'young calves meadow.' Miss Hermann operated the farm until she donated half of it to the Park System in 1969, and she donated the other half in 1973 (farm in 1969, lower right).

The Baysholm Tract protects the headwaters of a tributary of the Yellow Brook, which drains into the Swimming River Reservoir. The land is relatively flat and contains about 12.5 acres of wooded wetlands along the tributary. The remainder is about equally divided between leased farm fields and young forest that has grown up since farming was discontinued.

7. Durand Tract | 1969–90 ACRES; 2009–94 ACRES

IN THE SAME YEAR that Helen Hermann donated half of Baysholm Farm to the Park System, her Freehold Township neighbor one-half mile to the north, Elizabeth Durand, donated 90 acres of her farm on Randolph Road to the Park System, while retaining her residence on a separate lot. Freehold Township purchased 88 acres of adjacent farmland in 1984 and leased the Durand tract the following year from the Park System so that it could manage the entire 178 acres for conservation and passive recreation. Township officials established the Freehold Township Memorial Arboretum at Durand on 3.5 acres in 1991, and it has now grown to 33 acres. The Township also maintains a 20-acre Butterfly Meadow planted with native grasses and wildflowers to attract butterflies.

About 60% of the Durand Tract consists of old farm fields that are still farmed today. A 3.5-acre pond created around 1960 and the upper reaches of the Yellow Brook that flows through the Park provide some water habitat. The remainder of the land is forest that has grown up where farming was gradually abandoned in the second half of the 20th century.

8. East Freehold Showgrounds

1970–61 ACRES; 2009–81 ACRES

EAST FREEHOLD Showgrounds originated when Monmouth County purchased 160 acres of farmland on Kozloski Road to build administrative offices, and then transferred 61 acres that it didn't need to the Park System. In 1972, the Park System created the East Freehold Showgrounds with horse rings, shelters, and other facilities to accommodate the Monmouth County Horse Show, which had operated for a few years at Thompson Park, and other equestrian groups that needed an event site with easy access and ample parking. The 114th Monmouth County Horse Show in 2009 included some 600 riders and 700 horses and their owners, who arrived in campers, wagons, and trailers. They spent up to a week in the Park preparing and staging events in the three main horse rings, the jumper ring, hunter ring, and Grand Prix ring, where the 1st prize recipient won $30,000. Thousands of horse-lovers attended the show, which also raised money to benefit several non-profit groups.

The Monmouth County Fair moved to the Park in 1975, when the Park System agreed with the Monmouth County 4-H Association to co-sponsor it there. Agricultural fairs had taken place in the County intermittently at least as early as the 1850s, and the 4-H Association started running an annual Monmouth County Fair at Freehold High School in the 1950s. When the 4-H was looking

for a new place to hold the Fair, the East Freehold Showgrounds provided an ideal location, and collaboration with the Park System brought the Fair to a new level of public participation. More than 9,000 people attended the first fair at East Freehold in 1975 and more than 68,500 attended the 35th Fair there in 2009. Each year a Park System manager chairs the Fair, and many employees devote themselves to making the Fair one of the most popular events in the County.

The Park System hosted the Park's first dog show in 1982, and dog shows have grown increasingly popular there since. The Monmouth County Kennel Club's annual dog show on Memorial Day Weekend attracts thousands to the Park.

The County added 20 acres to the Park in 1983 and has planted shade trees and installed picnic tables that attract many visitors even when there are no events taking place. A tributary of the DeBois Creek, which drains to the Manasquan River, runs along the northern and western boundaries of the site. The Park's good soils and its proximity to the population center of Freehold Borough make it ideal for recreation.

9. Tatum Park | 1973–169 ACRES; 2009–366 ACRES

TATUM PARK began with a donation of 73 acres of Indian Springs Farm in Middletown by Genevieve Hubbard Tatum, the fourth Monmouth County woman within five years to donate her property for a County park. The Park System used a Federal Land and Water Conservation grant to purchase the remaining 97 acres of the farm. Victor "Bud" Grossinger, a four-term Freeholder and the first Chairman of the Board of Recreation Commissioners, had grown up on the farm and he worked closely with Mrs. Tatum (pictured below) on her donation.

Reverend Benjamin William Bennett, a pastor of the Middletown and Holmdel Baptist Churches, built the original farm house in the early 1800s. Bennett served for two terms as a U.S. Congressman and his son, William Bennett, later served as a Monmouth County Freeholder. After Captain John B. Story, who commanded six whaleboats operating off the Monmouth coast, acquired the property in 1852, it became known as Story Farm.

Mrs. Tatum's father-in-law, Charles Tatum, purchased the property in 1905 as a summer residence and named it Indian Springs Farm after a local legend about Indians using springs on the site. Tatum was president of the Whitall Tatum Company, which dated to 1806 and was the oldest glass manufacturer in the United States, with plants at Keyport in Monmouth County and Glassboro and Millville in South Jersey that made food and specimen jars. After Tatum died in 1920, his son Frederick Cooper Tatum became President of Whitall Tatum, and he and his wife

Genevieve moved into the house and expanded it. Bud Grossinger's father trained horses and ran the farm for the Tatums. The Park System converted the Tatum House into the Holland Activity Center, and offers a variety of popular programs and classes there including children's theater and dance, Chinese language, tai chi, yoga, aerobics, and pilates.

The Park System doubled the size of Tatum Park in the 1970s. The Federal Bureau of Recreation in 1974 transferred the 5-acre former U.S. Navy Middletown Radio Propagation Site on Red Hill Road to the Park System, which converted the building into the Red Hill Activity Center. The County purchased 41 acres of Brookside Farm from the Van Schoick Family in 1976, and acquired the 149-acre "Deepdale" tract with the help of the N. J. Conservation Foundation in 1979.

In 1980, the family of Bertha Heath (pictured below at dedication) donated funds to help establish the Clinton P. and Mary E. Heath Wing at the Red Hill Activity Center in honor of her parents and other members of the African American community of Red Hill in Middletown. Clinton Heath came from North Carolina in 1888 to work as a tenant

farmer and saved enough to buy a 50-acre farm on Harmony Road where he and his wife raised 13 children. Bertha, the youngest child, graduated from Middletown Township High School in 1926 and from the Harlem Hospital School of Nursing in 1930. She earned a degree in Public Health from New York University in 1948, a master's degree in Nursing from Columbia University in 1958, and worked in New York for 44 years as a nurse and nurse educator.

Tatum Park is located on the County's cuesta ridge and contains headwaters for Waackaack Creek, which drains to the Raritan Bay through Keansburg. The park today is about 75% forested, with an old growth forest of American beech and red and white oak in the southern hollows, and a late-succession forest of tulip poplar, sweet birch, and spicebush that has grown up on former fields and orchards. Old fields with native wildflowers provide habitat for birds, butterflies, and small mammals and the hawks that prey on them. The Park has more than six miles of trails, including one through a magnificent grove of American holly.

10. Shark River Golf Course | 1973-176 ACRES

IN THE EARLY 1800s the County established an Almshouse Farm for the poor on the site of Shark River Golf Course. The City of Asbury Park acquired the property in 1897 for a possible reservoir that was never completed. In 1918, Asbury Park commissioned the Scottish golf pro Joseph "Scotty" I'Anson to design the Asbury Park Golf and Country Club on the site as an amenity for its residents and many summer visitors. I'Anson created it as a "penal" course with hazards that "penalize" golfers who make errant shots. Back then golf course architects like I'Anson hit balls on partially completed courses to see where they went astray, and then placed hazards like bunkers where the balls landed.

The City used the course for victory gardens during the Second World War and leased it to a golf course operator in 1954. The extension of Route 18 in the 1960s cut off the southernmost portion of the course, requiring the redesign of some of its fairways and holes.

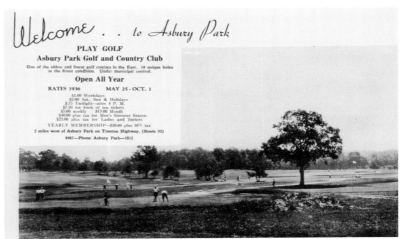

The Park System acquired the course in 1973 to preserve it from the proposed development of 2,000 houses on the site. Besides destroying the golf course, the intensive development would have threatened the forested wetlands along its 2.5 miles of frontage on the Jumping Brook and the Shark River.

Today, the Shark River Golf Course is one of the oldest golf courses in the County. In 2005, the Golf Maintenance staff researched the course's original "penal" design and restored portions of it that had been modified over the years. The 18-hole, par 71 course has a total length of 6,457 yards, and experienced golfers enjoy it for challenging and rewarding rounds of golf.

11. Hartshorne Woods Park

1973–46 ACRES; 2009–794 ACRES

HARTSHORNE Woods Park preserves nearly half of the unique Navesink Highlands, one of the highest areas along the Atlantic Coast and the County's most prominent natural feature. The name of the woods derives from Richard Hartshorne, a Middletown settler who accumulated more than 2,300 acres and settled on Portland Point on the Navesink River around 1680. Hartshorne descendants built homes along the river and on top of Rocky Point, the southeastern hill overlooking the river and the Atlantic. Artists like James Butterworth, whose painting is shown here, have long celebrated the Highlands' picturesque scenery, depicting what novelist James Fenimore Cooper called one of the most beautiful combinations of land and water in America.

The U.S. Army acquired 224 acres of the Highlands at the onset of World War II to build Battery Lewis to help defend New York harbor. As the Cold War developed, the Air Force built the Highlands Air Force Station west of the battery in 1948 for radar defense. The Army expanded the Station into the Highlands Army Air Defense Site, known as H.A.A.D.S., in 1958 to control Nike missile batteries around New York, including one in the Hilltop area of Holmdel Park.

The Federal Government cleared part of the property for the military installation, but left portions of the land in its natural state. When Park System officials learned in the mid-1960s that H.A.A.D.S. was becoming obsolete, they quickly communicated their interest in preserving the land as a County park. With grants from Green Acres and the Federal Open Space Program, the Park System bought nine private parcels within the Hartshorne Woods totaling 492 acres in 1973 and 1974. The U.S. Bureau of Outdoor Recreation transferred 161 acres of the Federal land to the County in 1974 through President Richard Nixon's Legacy of Parks program for surplus land. The U.S. General Services Administration transferred the 63-acre balance of the H.A.A.D.S. base to the County without cost in 1984.

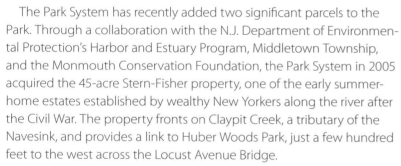

The Park System has recently added two significant parcels to the Park. Through a collaboration with the N.J. Department of Environmental Protection's Harbor and Estuary Program, Middletown Township, and the Monmouth Conservation Foundation, the Park System in 2005 acquired the 45-acre Stern-Fisher property, one of the early summer-home estates established by wealthy New Yorkers along the river after the Civil War. The property fronts on Claypit Creek, a tributary of the Navesink, and provides a link to Huber Woods Park, just a few hundred feet to the west across the Locust Avenue Bridge.

Daniel Ward Seitz, a descendant of Richard Hartshorne and a former president of the Friends of the Parks, bequeathed Portland Place, an ancestral home of the Hartshorne family, to the Park System when he died in 2008. Dan was a longtime supporter of the preservation of Hartshorne Woods and a co-founder of the Friends of the Parks. The five-acre property (pictured right) is one of the most important historic sites on the Navesink River. Thomas Hartshorne, Richard's grandson, may have built the oldest section of the house in the early 18th century, and his descendants and later owners expanded it several times. Park System staff are currently planning the use of this historic gem.

The elevation and steep slopes of the Navesink Highlands provided the best site in the region for guarding New York harbor at the outbreak of World War II. The U.S. Army built Battery Lewis in 1942 on the Highlands plateau in conjunction with Battery Harris at Fort Tilden on Rockaway Peninsula in New York to reinforce the primary battery at Fort Hancock on Sandy Hook. Battery Lewis was named for Colonel Isaac Newton Lewis, a West Point graduate who worked on New York Harbor defenses around 1900.

Battery Lewis contained two batteries. Battery 116 on top of the Highlands consists of a 600 ft.-long, 180 ft.-wide, and 40 ft.-high bunker built of densely reinforced concrete and covered with earth to withstand shells and aerial bombs. The bunker has two casemates, or fortified gun emplacements, protected by concrete canopies, and a long corridor between them with side rooms for generators, ammunition, and other uses. Each casemate sheltered a 16-in., 68 ft.-long gun capable of firing a 2,240 lb. armor-piercing projectile up to 25 miles. The 120-ton guns were originally cast for ships and were similar to the guns on the Battleship New Jersey.

Battery 219 on the east end of Rocky Point has a smaller bunker with casemates for two 6-in., 25-ft. long guns that were capable of firing projectiles 15 miles, plus ammunition and storage rooms. None of the Battery Lewis guns were ever fired in combat but nearby residents remembered test firings of the 16-in. guns that shook the ground and shattered windows. The Army deactivated Battery Lewis in 1949 and sold the guns for scrap.

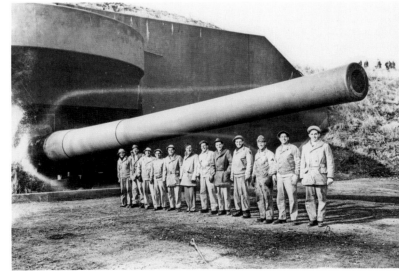

Hartshorne Woods Park contains almost 750 acres of forest at the eastern end of the cuesta ridge that extends from the Atlantic Highlands to western Monmouth County. The ridge's sedimentary rock separates New Jersey's inner and outer coastal plains, with the western slopes draining to the Raritan or New York Bays, and the eastern slopes draining to the Atlantic Ocean or the Delaware River.

The parkland's unique topography hosts old growth forest that has not been timbered since the 19th century and successional forest that has grown up on formerly cleared areas. The ridges have old growth forest of chestnut oak with an understory of huckleberry and blueberry. The slopes have a black, scarlet and chestnut oak forest with abundant mountain laurel that blooms strikingly in June. The protected hollows have an American beech-white oak-tulip poplar-hickory forest with a diverse understory, including mapleleaf and arrowwood viburnum. Formerly-occupied portions of Rocky Point have some significant American holly. American chestnut, which was decimated by disease a century ago, notably grows throughout the park and some 16-in. diameter specimens are among the largest in the region. Some rusted implements and open-grown trees within the Park indicate former farming and residential sites.

On the former H.A.A.D.S site, Park System ecologists and rangers have established grasslands for vistas and habitat. The Park provides some good habitat for species dependent on large forest blocks, including barred owl and pileated woodpeckers. The forested riverbanks provide unique habitat for osprey, kingfisher, and heron. Starting in the 1990s, volunteers have helped build and maintain more than 14 miles of trails in the Park for hikers, equestrians, all-terrain bicycles, cross-country skiers, and nature enthusiasts.

12. Mount Mitchill Scenic Overlook

1973–8 ACRES; 2009–12 ACRES

WITH an elevation of 266 feet, Mount Mitchill is the highest natural point along the North Atlantic Coast south of Maine. The site is named for Dr. Samuel Latham Mitchill, a physician, scientist, educator, and politician who measured its elevation with a barometer in 1816. Dr. Mitchill lived in New York and served in the House of Representatives and the Senate.

With its majestic view of Raritan Bay, Staten Island, Manhattan, Brooklyn, and Sandy Hook, Mount Mitchill has long been a popular viewing site, and in the 1940s there was an effort to make it a State park. A private refreshment stand and picnic area occupied one of several lots on the site for many years, but the area was mostly barren and unkempt. The sedimentary rock forming the Highlands is prone to slumping on steep slopes, where large blocks of capstone and sand periodically slide down the cliff face, and the lack of controls allowed considerable erosion.

A developer's proposal in the early 1970s to build two 15-story high-rise towers on the site prompted many calls for its preservation. The County tried to buy the entire site but the progress of the developer's plans raised the cost significantly. A compromise enabled the developer to build one tower and the County to preserve eight acres.

The Park System created the Mount Mitchill Scenic Overlook in 1973 with parking and viewing areas, drainage, and oak and cedar plantings to help control erosion along the steep slopes. In 1995, the Park System upgraded the Overlook with redesigned parking, viewing areas, interpretive panels, and landscaping (pictured above right in 1980, and center right in 1995).

Mount Mitchill first became a commemorative site in 1980 when the Park System installed flagpoles and a plaque paying homage to the eight soldiers who died during the U.S. Embassy hostage crisis in Iran.

In 2002, the Monmouth County 9/11 Memorial Committee chose Mount Mitchill for a memorial tribute to the victims and heroes of the attacks on the World Trade Center. The Committee and the Friends of the Parks raised several hundred thousand dollars for the memorial, and Freehold sculptor Franco Minervini carved an eagle for it with a 9-ft. wingspan ascending into flight while clutching a fragment of a steel beam from the World Trade Center. The granite base of the sculpture lists the names, ages, and towns of the 147 County natives and residents who lost their lives in the attacks, and the walkway to the memorial chronicles the timeline of the tragic event.

13. Huber Woods Park | 1974–119 ACRES; 2009–375 ACRES

HUBER WOODS PARK in the Locust section of Middletown was the fifth County park established by a family's generous donation of land. Four generations of the Huber family had enjoyed the Huber farm overlooking the Navesink River since Joseph Huber bought his first acreage on Brown's Dock Road in 1915. Huber's son and daughter-in-law, Hans and Catherine Huber, wanted to see 119 acres of woodland on the north end of their farm preserved in perpetuity as a nature sanctuary, and when they donated it in 1974, they specified that roads, playgrounds, recreational facilities, and powered recreational vehicles should be excluded from the property. They also requested that Brown's Dock Road along the west boundary of the land be maintained as a dirt road and not widened.

The Park System expanded the new Park that same year with the acquisition of 29 adjacent acres, and a year later Steven and Bonnie Wood donated three acres across Brown's Dock Road. With the assistance of the N.J. Conservation Foundation and a Green Acres matching grant, the Park System added 52 acres across from the Park in 1979.

In 1985, the Huber family generously donated the core of their farm estate on Brown's Dock Road, consisting of 48 acres with the Hans and Catherine Huber House, a barn and stable complex, and agricultural fields and woods sloping down to Navesink River Road. Huber family members had considered the development potential of the land but decided that they would rather see the farm preserved for light agricultural use and nature study.

The Park System made good use of the Huber Farm stables by moving the SPUR—Special People United to Ride—therapeutic riding program there in 1987 from Thompson Park, where there had been inadequate space. The Park System also turned the Huber House into an Environmental Center with hands-on and live animal exhibits and constructed an accessible Discovery path through the adjacent woods. In 1994, Park System carpenters erected an Activity Building made of logs next to the Environmental Center for educational programs and meetings. Park System naturalists conduct several popular programs at Huber Woods, including Creatures of the Night for Halloween visitors and building a Native American Longhouse for school and private groups.

In 2006, the County added a key parcel to the Park through the acquisition of the 99-acre Timolat Farm on Brown's Dock Road with the help of the Monmouth Conservation Foundation. James G. Timolat, who was originally from Staten Island and was President of the Oakland Chemical Company, purchased the property in 1909 and developed it into a country estate he named "Riverside." The acquisition consisted of the farm portion of the estate with a farmhouse, barns, and man-made ponds surrounded by old meadow and forest.

Settlers established farms on the north bank of the Navesink River by the middle of the 18th century, and typically built houses on the river and farmed the upland. Some also built docks for bringing in supplies and for shipping produce to New York. A farm owner named Brown built a dock on the front of his farm, and the road next to his farm became known as Brown's Dock Road. Members of the Brown family had farmed the land for more than 150 years when descendants sold 30 acres with river frontage in 1915 to Joseph M. Huber.

Joseph Huber came to New York in 1883 to sell dry color ink pigments that his family manufactured in Munich, Germany. He established J. M. Huber Corporation in New York in 1887 to manufacture and sell pigments, and soon after married Anna Gundlach, the daughter of German immigrants. Arriving by steam boat from Manhattan, Joseph and Anna rented Brown's peach farm on the Navesink in 1904 as a summer resi-

dence for their young family. Joseph brought his delivery wagon horses from the city to Brown's farm so that they could graze on the pasture.

The Hubers bought the Brown farm through the J. M. Huber Corporation in 1915 and built an Alpine-style house on the river. They acquired additional land up Brown's Dock Road, and their oldest son Hans and his wife Catherine Goss Huber built a larger Alpine-style house on the hill in 1927. They spent summers there with their six children, farming the land with hay and corn for their horses, cows, chickens, and pigs and producing milk, butter, and eggs for themselves and neighbors.

After Hans and Catherine died, everyone in the family remembered how much they enjoyed the property and wanted to see it preserved. As Michael Huber recalled, a cousin summed up the family sentiment in a letter, writing that "she would love to see the farm used as a place where city kids could come and learn about nature."

Huber Woods Park occupies a lower elevation of the County's cuesta ridge to the west of the Navesink Highlands and Hartshorne Woods Park. The historical use of the parkland was equally divided between woods and pasture and orchards, but today about four-fifths, or 300 acres, is forested. The older woods on the ridges resemble those of Hartshorne Woods Park, with mixed oak and chestnut, including some remnant American chestnut, with an understory of mountain laurel. Tulip poplar forests have grown up on long-abandoned pastures, while eastern red cedar woodlands are found on more recently-abandoned fields. Norway spruce groves planted by the Huber and Timolat families thrive near the Environmental Center and further west on the former Timolat Farm.

The wooded areas of the Park host pileated woodpeckers, great horned owls, and scarlet tanager. Birds hunting over the fields include raptors like bald eagle, American kestrel, red-shouldered hawk, red-tailed hawk, and non-raptors such as black and turkey vultures and swallow-tailed kite. Songbirds that flock to the feeders, gardens, and fields include pine siskin, eastern bluebird, Carolina chickadee, American goldfinch, indigo bunting, and Baltimore oriole.

The five ponds on the former Timolat Farm provide habitat for several water birds, including wood duck, Wilson's snipe, gadwall, ringed-neck ducks, hooded merganser, black ducks, and green and great blue herons. Wood frogs and spring peepers fill the area around the ponds with calls each spring.

The Park System manages the 75 acres of fields as pasture for horses and as old fields enhanced with wildflowers to preserve a pastoral landscape of rolling hills and tree-lined fencerows with intermittent views of the Navesink River. The success of the 8.5 miles of trails that Park ecologists and rangers developed in 1991 for casual walkers, hikers, and equestrians has provided a model for developing trails in Hartshorne Woods and other parks.

14. Hominy Hill Golf Course

1977–183 ACRES; 2009–262 ACRES

WHEN Henry Dickson Mercer, Sr., built Hominy Hill in 1965, it was one of New Jersey's most exclusive private golf courses, and since the Park System acquired it in 1977, it has often been rated as New Jersey's #1 public golf course in national and regional publications.

Henry Mercer was president of the States Marine Corporation, a shipping company, and lived in Rumson. He purchased several farms in Colts Neck in 1941 to raise prize-winning herds of Guernsey cattle. He eventually accumulated 411 acres and named his land Hominy Hill Farm after the Manhomoney Hills, the historic name for a group of small hills in the Colts Neck area.

In 1963, Mr. Mercer commissioned the famed golf course architect, Robert Trent Jones, Sr., of Montclair, N.J., to convert 180 acres of the farm into an 18-hole golf course for entertaining his many foreign business contacts when they visited New York. Jones designed or redesigned hundreds of challenging courses during his seven-decade career with the philosophy that golfers had to earn their rewards through high achievement. Mr. Mercer directed Jones to spare no expense in making Hominy Hill a championship-quality golf course. Jones

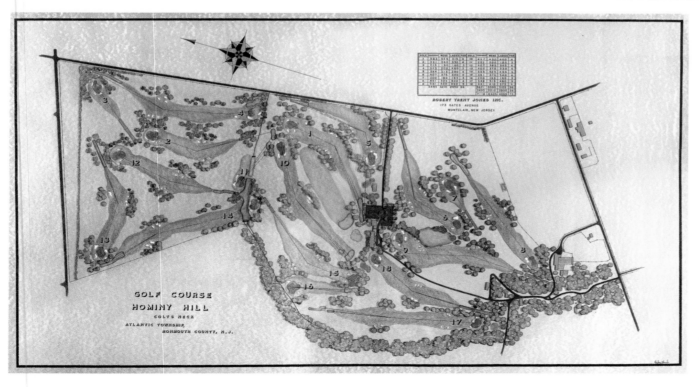

GOLF COURSE
HOMINY HILL
COLTS NECK
ATLANTIC TOWNSHIP,
MONMOUTH COUNTY, N.J.

laid out a long par 72 course measuring 7,120 yards and installed 138 bunkers to challenge golfers, and he incorporated tributaries of the Mine Brook that runs through the rolling landscape as water hazards on several holes.

Mr. Mercer hired architect Derrick Kipp to convert the farm's large dairy barn into a well-appointed clubhouse with locker rooms and an informal restaurant with seating for 60 people on the ground floor. He turned the enormous hayloft into a formal restaurant with seating for 125 people and a large kitchen. In spite of its lavish features and meticulous care, few people actually got the opportunity to play golf at Hominy Hill. Mr. Mercer occasionally opened the course to charity events, but otherwise golfers played there only by invitation. He missed seeing cattle on the remaining portion of the farm, and he started a purebred Charolais beef cattle herd there.

The Mercer family decided to put the course up for sale in 1975 and made a verbal agreement to sell it to the County. The Mercers resisted offers from developers to purchase the course at a higher price during the 18 months it took for the Park System to secure a Green Acres matching grant for the acquisition. While some people were concerned that the Park System would not be able to maintain Hominy Hill at the level of quality that the Mercers had achieved, the popularity of the course since its acquisition has long silenced any skeptics. In 2010, readers of *New Jersey Monthly* magazine named Hominy Hill as their favorite public golf course in the State.

Dave Pease, the Park System's Manager of Golf Courses, started working at Hominy Hill soon after the County acquired it in the spring of 1977, and he recalled in a 2004 interview, "The golfers were extremely excited about playing at Hominy Hill because now they had access to something that was previously closed to them, and they continued being excited." By the end of its first year of operation, Hominy Hill had become the Park System's largest source of revenue, exceeding both Shark River and Howell Park Golf Courses.

Over the years Park System golf staff have made a number of improvements to the greens and fairways for more active use of the course, and in a national recognition of the quality of Hominy Hill and the Park System's operation of it, the U.S. Golf Association held its 58th U.S. Amateur Public Links Championship on the course in 1983. The USGA held its 19th U.S. Women's Amateur Public Links Championship at Hominy Hill in 1995, and the chairwoman of the event said it was the finest of all the 19 that the organization had sponsored.

Since 1993, the Friends of the Parks have held an annual Friends Golf Tournament at Hominy Hill to support the Park System's Junior Golf Program and other programs. Forty players participated in the 1993 tournament and corporate sponsors and private donors contributed over $7,000 to the effort. The Friends raised nearly $18,000 at their 2009 Tournament.

HOMINY HILL
GOLF COURSE

15. Deep Cut Gardens | 1977–39 ACRES; 2009–54 ACRES

DEEP CUT GARDENS is Monmouth County's horticultural park dedicated to home gardeners, and it was the sixth County Park to be established by a major land donation and the fifth by a woman. The land has a long history of cultivation dating back to the late 17th century, when settlers established the nearby village of Middletown and cleared surrounding land for crops and pasture. Edward and Teresa R. Dangler bought a 35-acre farm parcel in 1925 and erected a 10-room Colonial Revival mansion on the promontory off Red Hill Road that affords picturesque views of the Highlands. The Danglers landscaped the hillside and planted many fruit trees.

In 1935, Vito Genovese, a New York mobster, purchased the property and moved there with his wife and three children. Genovese expanded the house and refashioned the estate to remind him of Naples, Italy, where he was born. He had previously lived in Atlantic Highlands and he hired the Caruso Construction Company, which was known for building the huge retaining walls there, to do the landscape and building work. Caruso subcontracted with the famous J.T. Lovett Monmouth Nursery of Little Silver to design and plant the gardens. Lovett's landscape architect, Theodore Stoudt (pictured below), who graduated from Penn State, designed the gardens with Italian and English features, including a rockery with terraced pools, a walled parterre with boxwood and roses, and a stone gazebo at the east end.

At Genovese's request, Caruso built a "Mt. Vesuvius" pseudo-volcano that erupted with smoke during parties. Genovese installed a swimming pool, a tennis court, a playground, and a three-hole golf course, and constructed a greenhouse and a garage with gardener's quarters. After he fled to Italy in 1937 to escape a murder charge, a mysterious fire destroyed the house. Dominic Caruso acquired the property in 1948 to satisfy liens from the construction.

In 1953, Karl and Marjorie Sperry Wihtol purchased "Deep Cut Farm," as the property had become known, and erected a one-story ranch house on the site of the previous house. Mrs. Wihtol was the daughter of Alexander Sperry, co-founder of Sperry and Hutchinson, the trading stamps company. She studied at Columbia University and the Sorbonne in Paris. A well-known book lover, Mrs. Wihtol served for many years as the president of the Middletown Library and she established a scholarship fund there for local students interested in studying library science. She was also an avid horticulturist and she restored the greenhouse at Deep Cut and grew succulents there that she collected from fellow enthusiasts in the United States, Britain, South America, and South Africa.

The Wihtols restored the rockery and gardens, planted ornamental trees, and installed a pool on the west side of the house. When Mrs. Wihtol died in 1977, she bequeathed half the property to the County for park and horticultural purposes, and the Park System used a Green Acres matching grant to purchase the rest. With the help of the Monmouth Conservation Foundation, the Park System in 1990 acquired 13 adjacent acres that had been slated for an eight-lot subdivision.

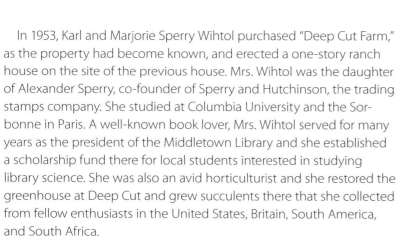

When the Park System took over Deep Cut Farm, staff members uncovered the formal gardens that had become overgrown and restored the greenhouse and gazebo. They adapted the Wihtol house into a Horticultural Center with two classrooms, a horticultural library, a gift shop for hard-to-find plants and gardening items, a kitchen, and offices. They converted the Wihtol swimming pool into a 'water garden' pond, and planted a number of specimen trees.

The Park System named the new park Deep Cut Gardens and opened it in 1978 with horticulturist Margaret 'Peggy' Crooks, who for many years was the Garden Editor for the *Asbury Park Press*, as Garden Center Director. Staff gardeners planted demonstration plots, propagated special plants in the greenhouse, and presented horticultural programs for home gardeners. Mrs. Crooks started a Friends of the Garden volunteer program which was a forerunner of the Friends of the Parks. Elvin McDonald of New York donated about 1,000 books to the Deep Cut library, which the Park System named the Elvin McDonald Horticultural Library in his honor.

Between 2005 and 2008, the Park System restored the large parterre at Deep Cut, repairing the stone walls and recreating the patterned flower beds of the original garden. In 2009, Park System ecologists and Deep Cut staff launched a plan using the gardens and fields to educate the public about environmentally sound horticultural practices and about New Jersey's native plant communities. They have established several planting areas as demonstration sites for re-establishing native species.

On the east side of the formal gardens, the ecologists planted three groves: an oak grove to illustrate the type of woodland that grows on dry and sandy soils, a maple grove to illustrate woodland on well-drained soils, and an ash grove to illustrate woodland on moderately-drained soils. Between the groves are glades of low grasses and wildflowers. In the successional woodlands around the boundaries that comprise a little more than half the park, the ecologists are controlling or removing invasive species to allow native species to regenerate naturally.

16. Seven Presidents Oceanfront Park

1977–33 ACRES; 2009–38 ACRES

THE SITE and name of Seven Presidents Oceanfront Park is linked with Long Branch's history as a fashionable East Coast seashore resort. President Ulysses S. Grant began the presidential tradition in 1869 when he rented a cottage in Long Branch and made it the nation's "summer capital." Presidents Rutherford B. Hayes, James A. Garfield, Chester A. Arthur, Benjamin Harrison, William McKinley, and Woodrow Wilson all spent part of their vacations in Long Branch during their terms.

Many wealthy businessmen and celebrities visited Long Branch during its heyday, including entertainers like William "Buffalo Bill" Cody and Annie Oakley. A showman named Nate Salsbury became a partner in Cody's enormously popular Wild West Show in 1884, and in the 1890s he built a seaside compound with a thousand feet of oceanfront in Long Branch and called it the "Reservation." Along the "Trail" though the Reservation, he built nine large cottages in the Shingle and Queen Anne Styles and named them for Indian tribes (drawing at right). Cody and his troupe of Indians, sharpshooters, and bareback riders spent time in Long Branch while they performed in New Jersey cities and in New York and Philadelphia, and the cottages became known as the Buffalo Bill Cody houses, even though Buffalo Bill himself never owned one.

After the area fell into decline, the City of Long Branch started acquiring parts of the former Reservation in 1973 and commissioned plans to create Seven Presidents Oceanfront Park there. By mutual agreement, the Park System assumed responsibility in 1977 for operating the 33-acre park since it attracted regional visitation. Long Branch transferred the Park to the Park System in 1984. Only one of the Reservation's cottages, "Navaho," remained, and the Park System moved it to the north end of the Park and renovated it for park use (pictured above right in 1978, prior to park improvements).

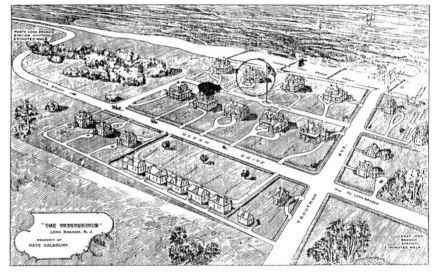

The Park System improved the beach and facilities at Seven Presidents Oceanfront Park in the early 1980s with grants from Green Acres and the Federal Land and Water Conservation Fund. When annual visitation passed 500,000 in the mid-1990s, the Park System acquired more land for parking and additional recreation facilities. In 2005, the Park System opened a 4½-acre Skateplex on the north end of the Park with a skate-bowl and a street course with quarter pipes, ramps, and funboxes for beginning, intermediate, and advanced skateboarders. The Skateplex also includes an in-line skating rink, a paved trail, and a shelter.

In 2009, a multi-year collaboration between the Park System, Challenged Youth Sports of Middletown, and the Friends of the Parks came to fruition with the opening of Tony's Place, an accessible playground for children of all ages and abilities to play and interact. Tony's Place is named in honor of the late Anthony Musella, a Middletown dentist and former Vice Chairman of the Board of Recreation Commissioners, who had volunteered much time helping children with special needs to enjoy sports activities.

The Park System manages the Park to balance its intensive beach recreation with conservation of its littoral environment. Staff ecologists and rangers restored the eroded dunes in 1983, and have maintained and expanded them over the years. American beachgrass, bayberry, and beach plum shrubs now help secure the ocean side of the dune. The land side hosts a stunted woodland community of red cedar, black cherry, and vines, especially poison ivy. The staff also established 'natural areas' on the seaward side of the dunes, where seashells and other natural debris now provide rare habitat for some threatened and endangered species like the small annual seabeach amaranth and shorebirds such as the least tern and piping plover, which nest in the sand and have successfully fledged chicks each year.

17. Clayton Park |

THE CLAYTON FARM in Upper Freehold Township remarkably survived into the late 20th century as one of the County's best-preserved historic rural landscapes. Paul Clayton had farmed the land from the time of his purchase in 1906 until he retired in 1972 at the age of 87. Paul and his daughter Thelma lived in their 1840s farmhouse without plumbing, electricity, or telephone, and they pumped water from a well outside the back door. Paul farmed with horses until his son helped him with a tractor for the last few years (farmhouse above right in 1982; below are Paul Clayton and daughter Thelma, right in photo).

Doctor's Creek runs in a deep ravine through the farm's majestic woods, and lumbermen pestered the Claytons for years to log them. The high ground affords panoramic views of the Upper Freehold farmlands, and developers tried to buy the farm to subdivide it. Instead, the Claytons chose to sell their land to the County to preserve it, and they held on for five years while Park System staff secured financing with help from the N.J. Conservation Foundation and Green Acres. The Park System purchased the farm in 1979 and the Claytons donated a six-acre woodlot in 1982.

In 1990, two years before Paul died at 107, Thelma told a *Newark Star Ledger* reporter (August 18, 1990), "Monmouth County was all agricultural years ago. Then to see so much development— it looks quite sad. There were so many beautiful farms then and now they're all gone…We sold to the county by choice. We didn't want the farm torn up. We had many happy days there as a family. We wanted the happiness to stay so the children of tomorrow could be happy too."

Clayton Park lies on the western end of the cuesta ridge that extends to Hartshorne Woods Park, and it was the Park System's first large land acquisition in the rural western part of the County. From a high elevation of 240 feet, the parkland slopes down to 110 feet at the lowest level of Doctor's Creek, which drains to Crosswicks Creek, a tributary of the Delaware River.

Due to better soil and moisture conditions, the Piedmont environment typically hosts more species than those found on the outer coastal plain. Because the Clayton woods have not been logged for many decades, they contain some of highest quality hardwood forest in the County. The old growth woods are dominated by American beech, white and red oak, and birch trees and have a diverse and lush understory. Black oak, white and green ash, tulip poplar, and shagbark hickory trees are also plentiful. An 18-acre field released from agriculture in the 1950s shows the successional transition from the pioneer red cedar trees to the tulip poplars and oaks that now dominate them.

A small man-made pond at the intersection of forest and fields provides some interesting edge habitat for many species, including beaver, turtles, and wading birds like egrets, heron, and snow geese. The forest and field juncture also provides habitat for quail, pheasant, and wild turkey. Spice bush and greenbriar shrubs and skunk cabbage thrive in wet areas. Interesting perennials include strawberry bush, beechdrops, rattlesnake plant, roundlobe hepatica, hobblebush, American golden saxifrage, trumpet vine, ladyfern, and cinnamon fern. Six miles of trails through Clayton Park provide access to some of the best forest landscapes and spring wildflower sites in the County.

18. Weltz Park | 1979–114 ACRES; 2009–165 ACRES

BY THE 1970s, the Weltz Farm in Ocean Township was one of the last remaining large tracts of open space east of Route 35 in southern Monmouth County. Samuel and Louise Weltz purchased their 114-acre farm in 1944, and had held on to it while most of the surrounding area was developed. Four acres along Route 35 were zoned commercial and the remaining land had the potential for 186 house lots. Members of the Ocean Township Environmental Commission urged County officials to preserve the land, noting the abundant wildlife by the farm pond and along Whalepond Brook, which runs to the Atlantic.

The Weltzes also wanted the land preserved and they sold the property below its appraised value to N.J. Conservation Foundation, which held it until the Park System could secure a Green Acres matching grant. The Foundation also helped add 29 acres to the Park in 1979, and the Park System acquired another 22 acres in 1984, which extended the Park into Eatontown. In the 1990s, a coalition of local citizens requested that the Park remain undeveloped for passive recreation.

The Park has 44 acres of intermediate upland forest that is typical of the Pine Barrens, with white, black, red, and chestnut oaks and pitch pines, and 52 acres of wetter lowland forests, with red maple, gray birch, sweetgum, and Atlantic white cedar. Although five miles inland, the Park's 57 acres of sandy and dry fields provide habitat for coastal dune species like beach heather and prickly pear shrubs. Juniper and bayberry shrubs also thrive in the sandy fields, along with butterfly milkweed and many native grasses. Twelve acres of scrub and shrub land host bayberry, sumac, alder, and other small trees and shrubs that provide good bird habitats. Rows of highbush blueberries under a young woodland canopy illustrate the adaptation of a blueberry field to the successional forest. Two miles of trails through the woods and fields provide good vantages for watching birds and butterflies.

19. Pine Brook Golf Course | 1981–61 ACRES

PINE BROOK Golf Course is the seventh County recreation facility established by a major donation of land. Hovnanian Enterprises of Red Bank built the Covered Bridge adult community of 1,780 homes in Manalapan Township with the Pine Brook Golf Course as one of its primary amenities. Pine Brook is an 18-hole, executive-length golf course with shorter fairways than a standard golf course. Its donation has enabled the Park System to provide playing opportunities for golfers who prefer shorter and faster rounds. Pine Brook was also the Park System's first golf course in the west-central portion of the County.

The noted golf course architect Hal Purdy designed Pine Brook for Hovnanian, which first opened it in 1975. Purdy, who designed nearly 50 golf courses in his career, laid out the par 61, 4,168-yard course in a broad arc along Pine Brook, which drains to the Matchaponix Brook in the Raritan River watershed. Hovnanian's donation included a two-story clubhouse with a manager's office, a maintenance building, and parking.

20. Historic Walnford | 1985–36 ACRES

WALNFORD is one of New Jersey's premier historic sites and the eighth County park established by a generous gift of land. Edward and Joanne Mullen donated Walnford with 36 acres in 1979, and it is now the centerpiece of the 1,479-acre Crosswicks Creek Greenway.

Walnford remains remarkably intact as a farm and mill complex spanning three centuries, thanks to its isolation and continuous tenure by one family for over 200 years, and many extant documents illuminate its fascinating history. Like many colonial settlements, Walnford originated as a mill site, and it functioned as a small milling village for more than 100 years. In 1734, Samuel Rodgers, a merchant in nearby Allentown, bought 323 acres of land that included the Walnford site and erected a dam, grist mill, two-story brick house, shops, and barns, all of which are now gone. Rogers sold his "pleasantly situated plantation" with 173 acres in 1750, and it passed through several owners over the next two decades.

Richard Waln, a prominent Philadelphia Quaker merchant, bought the plantation in 1772, beginning more than 200 years of ownership by the Waln/Meirs family. Waln built the Georgian Style house in 1773 and named the plantation Walnford. His journals document colonial trade, as he shipped flour, grains, hams, lumber, and other Walnford products down the Crosswicks Creek and Delaware River to Philadelphia and to distant ports. Waln's son Nicholas inherited the property in 1809 and rebuilt the grist mill after it burned in 1821. When his daughter, Sarah Waln Hendrickson, succeeded him, she updated the house, built an imposing carriage house, and reconstructed the grist mill again after another fire in 1872.

In 1907, the property passed to Richard Waln Meirs, the grandson of Sarah's brother. Meirs and his wife Anne Weightman Meirs used the property as a summer home, and Anne closed the grist mill after her husband died in 1917. Their son William Meirs inherited 41 acres with the house, barns, and mill in 1958 and maintained the property while he lived in Philadelphia (carriage house and mill at right in the 1970s). After a suspicious fire destroyed the two early tenant houses pictured below in 1969, Meirs decided to put the property up for sale. Aware of the site's important history and historic buildings, Park System officials wanted to preserve it as a County park but didn't have the funding to do so.

Ed and Joanne Mullen (bottom right) bought Walnford in 1973 for their large family. When they moved in a year later, it was the first time the house had been lived in full time in nearly 70 years. The Mullens researched Walnford's history, interviewed William Meirs on his family's ownership, collected historic photographs, and nominated the property to the National Register of Historic Places. After enjoying Walnford for seven years, they decided to donate it to the County for long-term preservation. Along with the property, the Mullens donated some Waln and Meirs furnishings and household items that they had acquired when they purchased Walnford.

In a 2004 oral history interview with the Mullens, Ed said, "We enjoyed living here. Walnford opened our eyes to New Jersey history." Joanne added, "It's a good feeling to know that it's being so well taken care of and that so many people are able to come and visit and enjoy it."

The Waln house is the largest surviving pre-Revolutionary house in Monmouth County. In keeping with their Quaker traditions, Richard and Elizabeth Waln built a substantial but unpretentious house in the Georgian Style using lumber from the sawmill on the property. With a wide center hall, generously proportioned rooms, and tall ceilings, the Waln house epitomized a gracious country house in the Delaware Valley on the eve of the Revolutionary War.

In the 19th century, Waln descendants updated the porch and cornice, added a store wing on the west side, and installed marble fireplaces on the interior. When Waln's great, great grandson, Richard Waln Meirs, and his wife Anne transformed Walnford into a country estate in the early 20th century, they renovated the house in the Colonial Revival Style, installed plumbing, electricity, and central heating for the first time, and added a caretaker's wing. When Ed and Joanne Mullen purchased Walnford in 1973, they stabilized the mill, replaced roofs, modernized mechanical systems, and installed a modern kitchen in the house, but otherwise preserved the property intact.

With funding from the County of Monmouth and grants from the New Jersey Historic Trust, the Park System completed restoration of Walnford's major buildings in 2000, including the house, mill, carriage house, and cow barn. The Park System restored the Waln house to its appearance in 1915, after Richard and Anne Meirs made the last major alterations. The Friends of the Parks generously supported the reproductions of wallpaper and furniture for the house and the fabrication of interpretive exhibits.

Waln's Mill, built in 1873, is the only operating gristmill remaining in Monmouth County, and one of only a handful in the State. In a 1981 report to the Park System, Charles Howell, an English millwright and master miller at Phillipsburg Manor in Tarrytown, N.Y., wrote, "The mill machinery layout is a perfect example of a water-powered country flour and gristmill of the 1870s. The mill is probably one of the best surviving examples of a complete millstone mill in the eastern United States and possibly in the whole of the country. Restoring this mill to working order will be a wonderful asset to Monmouth County, and indeed, to New Jersey. The educational value to young and old alike will be immense."

The Park System opened the restored grist mill in 1997 and a year later began operating the machinery for the first time since 1917. To enhance Walnford's historic setting, the Park System obtained permission from Upper Freehold Township to vacate the portion of Walnford Road that runs through the Park along Crosswicks Creek.

The farm and mill complex is perched on a narrow ridge bound by Shoppen Run to the north and Crosswicks Creek and its floodplain to the south and west. While most of Monmouth County drains to the Raritan Bay or the Atlantic, Crosswicks Creek drains into the Delaware River. The plant communities at Walnford reflect the area's rich Piedmont soils and include notable species like Virginia bluebells, which carpet parts of the floodplain in the spring, and the majestic American sycamores, with their distinctive white bark, that grow along the stream banks.

21. Dorbrook Recreation Area

1985–381 ACRES; 2009–535 ACRES

WITH its prime location, easy access, and multiple activities, the Dorbrook Recreation Area on Route 537 in Colts Neck Township is the Park System's most heavily scheduled area for recreational programs. When the County acquired the 381-acre Dorbrook Farm in 1985 with a Green Acres matching grant, much of the land had been farmed for well over 200 years. Murray Rosenberg, the president of the Miles Shoe Company of New York, bought the 80-acre Atlantic Stock Farm in 1937 to create a country estate for his family, and he named it Dorbrook Farm (pictured right in the 1950s). Rosenberg built a house and renovated the existing barns so he could raise prize-winning cattle. Over time he added several adjacent parcels, including the Polhemus Farm, which includes an early 19th century farmhouse that the Park System has preserved.

The large size of Dorbrook, its level terrain, and its frontage on the Swimming River Reservoir has enabled the Park System to simultaneously protect regional water supply, preserve prime farmland, and develop multiple recreational opportunities. In 1994, the Park System added the 130-acre Festoon Farm, an adjacent farm formerly owned by the Nathan family.

Visitor Services staff use the former Dorbrook and Festoon homes as venues for a wide variety programs and classes, including parent and child programs, summer camps, therapeutic recreation, cooking, fitness, and yoga. In addition to expansive playing fields for a variety of sports, the Park includes two swimming pools, tennis and basketball courts, and an in-line skating rink, and the staff offers instructions in most of these activities. With help from Challenged Youth Sports of Middletown and the Friends of the Parks, the Park System created the Challenger Place universally-accessible playground in 2004, and the same year it added the Sprayground, a water-enhanced playground.

DORBROOK
RECREATION AREA

The Dorbrook Recreation Area is nestled among surviving orchards and horse farms that once dominated eastern Monmouth County. The Park protects nearly one mile of frontage on the Swimming River Reservoir. About three-quarters of the park is open land, with 100 acres of recreational and buffer areas near Route 537 and almost 300 acres of grassland and leased agricultural fields. Mature forest and hedgerows cover about 130 acres. Park System ecologists established the grassland areas in 2002 on former agricultural fields by allowing native cover to grow with one annual mowing. Most of this acreage has developed herbaceous wetland characteristics and in some areas vernal pools form in the spring and provide ephemeral habitat for many species.

The varied cover between tall and short grasses, agricultural ground, herbaceous wetland, and vernal pools provides habitats for field nesting species, including some species of concern, that are dependent on extensive and diverse cover types. Ecologists have observed the State-endangered northern harrier and loggerhead

strike utilizing the fields for hunting, and the State-threatened bobolink using them for breeding, as well as black-necked stilt and eastern meadowlark. A popular 2.3-mile paved trail provides interesting views of the varied field cover along the edge of the narrow forest that borders the reservoir. The Park System has developed the intense active recreation at Dorbrook to coexist harmoniously with its natural areas and agricultural fields.

22. Bayshore Waterfront Park

1988–8 ACRES; 2009–227 ACRES

THE PARK SYSTEM realized a long-term goal to establish a County park on Sandy Hook Bay when it acquired eight acres in Port Monmouth from the Conservation Fund in 1988 (future park area pictured at right in the 1980s). Since then the Park System has consolidated 90 lots into Bayshore Waterfront Park, preserving a valuable coastal landscape from intense bayshore development and providing almost a mile of public access along the bay.

Settlers established Shoal Harbor, the historical name of the Port Monmouth area, in the late 17th century. The Seabrook-Wilson House, one of the oldest houses on the Bayshore and a local landmark rich in community and maritime history, became part of the Park in 1998 in a land transfer with Middletown Township. Daniel Seabrook acquired 202 acres on the Bayshore in 1696, and his son or grandson built the oldest section of the house in the early 1700s. After five generations as a Seabrook family farm, William V. Wilson purchased the farm in 1855 and lived there with his family until the turn of the century. Several owners operated the house as an inn during the 20th century under names like the Bay Side Manor and the White House Tavern.

By the late 1960s the house had become dilapidated and vacant. At the urging of local residents concerned about its preservation, Middletown Township acquired the property in 1969, and a local historical association operated it as the Spy House Museum. Restored by the Park System in 2009, the building is now used for Park System programs, with exhibits under development on the history and ecology of the Bayshore. The Park includes a 300-ft. fishing pier, a favorite of local fishermen, and attracts kayakers, windsurfers, birders, beachcombers, and other visitors who enjoy the spectacular bay views.

Bayshore Waterfront Park contains the largest intact estuarine marshes in Sandy Hook Bay and includes coastal wetland, deciduous maritime shrublands, and two tidal creeks, Compton's Creek and Pews Creek, which drain small upland watersheds. The plant community in these estuaries is highly influenced by the level of salinity in different areas. Smooth cordgrass adapted to higher salt concentrations dominates the low salt marsh, which receives regular inundation of tidal water. Saltmeadow cordgrass adapted to lower salinity dominates the high salt marsh, which receives an occasional inundation.

Meandering tidal creeks like these pulse with the tides in and out of the estuary, carrying nutrients and multitudes of marine organisms that interact with the grasses. Channels dug in the mid-20th century to expose mosquito populations to fish predators have increased the efficiency of the flow, but they have also reduced shallow pooled areas, called pans, that support species like sea lavender and glasswort and provide feeding areas for many bird species. Some undisturbed meandering channels can still be detected, and as the old linear channels gradually fill in, the meanders and pools are beginning to return.

Estuaries such as these at Bayshore Waterfront Park are some of the most productive ecosystems on earth. With each tide, life is flushed in and out of these rich landscapes. Many notable species such as northern harrier, great blue and yellow-crowned night heron, American oystercatcher (pictured at right), black skimmer, and osprey feed and nest in this landscape. The marsh is filled with fiddler crabs, ribbed mussels, pulmonate snails, and dozens of other species that support the marine ecology of Sandy Hook Bay and beyond.

23. Manasquan Reservoir

1988–1,052 ACRES; 2009–1,204 ACRES

THE OPENING of the Manasquan Reservoir in Howell Township in 1990 realized 30 years of planning by County and State officials to create a water storage facility for southern Monmouth County "with full utilization of its recreational potential." The Park System assumed recreational management of the 1,052-acre reservoir site from the N.J. Water Supply Authority and opened it initially for boating and fishing on the 770-acre reservoir and hiking and biking on the 282 acres around it. In its first full year of operation in 1991, the reservoir attracted over 128,000 visitors and recorded 2,000 boat launchings.

In 1994, the Park System opened a Visitor Center (pictured above) on the south shore of the lake with a fishing pier, a launching ramp for sailboats and boats with electric motors, and kayak and rowboat rentals. The Visitor Center also has an observation deck and a "wildlife" playground highlighting species in the reservoir habitat. Park staff use electric-powered pontoon boats for reservoir tours about surface water sources and the Park's wildlife, including looking for herons, osprey, and bald eagles. When ice conditions permit, park rangers open the reservoir in the winter for ice skating, ice boating, and ice fishing.

The original planners of the reservoir designated a site on the west shore for environmental education, and the Park System opened the Manasquan Reservoir Environmental Center in 2001. The Environmental Center focuses on wetlands ecology and wildlife conservation, and includes hands-on exhibits, classroom and program space, and indoor and outdoor wildlife observation areas. A simulated wetland at the entrance provides multiple opportunities for observation and guided learning. Naturalists present a variety of programs at the Center for school groups and other visitors about wetlands, protecting water supply, and the local wildlife.

The Cove Trail next to the Environmental Center enables visitors to walk through a wetland, and the Park's five-mile Perimeter Trail provides a scenic route around the reservoir for hikers, bikers, joggers, and equestrians. The combination of water, wildlife, and recreation opportunities has made the Manasquan Reservoir the Park System's most visited park, attracting more than 1.2 million people in 2009.

Creation of the Manasquan Reservoir to provide water for the growing shore population had a huge impact on the reservoir site and on the watershed below it. The site was ideal for the purpose as it consisted of a large forested wetland in the upper Manasquan River watershed where it was protected from any adjacent run-off. The reservoir collects rainwater that falls on it, and a downstream pumping station on the river pumps water to the reservoir when it is available.

The reservoir construction (pictured below) flooded most of the site's former deciduous forest wetland. The forest that remains around the water is mostly upland, composed of mixed oak-chestnut oak communities with some red maple and black gum in the wetter areas. The Bear Swamp tract to the southeast contains primarily pitch pine and is the unflooded remnant of the former forested wetland. The forests in the park remain relatively undisturbed by invasive species. The Eastern turkey beard has been found in the pitch pine lowlands and is the only known population of that perennial within the County parks. The southern twayblade, a diminutive orchid measuring only three to four inches in height, is a State-imperiled species that is also unique to the Park.

As the largest freshwater lake in the area, the reservoir has become an important habitat for many bird species, most notably American bald eagles (pictured left). An immature eagle was first noticed in 2001, and a nesting pair fledged two chicks in 2002 and in 2003, and three in 2004. When the first female died while nesting in 2005, a second replaced her in 2006 and the nesting pair fledged two chicks each year in 2007–2009. One of the 2007 chicks was an eaglet rehabilitated after being injured when a storm destroyed its nest in the Blackwater National Wildlife Refuge on the eastern shore of Maryland. Although workers cleared many acres of the former forest for the grading and flooding of the reservoir, they left trees in some areas that died following inundation, and these have provided excellent snag (dead tree) habitats for the eagles and for ospreys (pictured right). They also provide microhabitats that protect fish and invertebrate water species from elements and predators.

24. Henry Hudson Trail | 1990–9 MILES; 2009–22 MILES

TO PRESERVE the right-of-way of the former Bayshore rail corridor, County officials secured a State grant in 1980 to acquire it from Conrail. The Central Railroad of New Jersey had built the rail line in the 19th century to serve the towns along the Sandy Hook Bay from Aberdeen to Atlantic Highlands. In response to the growing interest in trails, the Park System assumed management of nine miles of the right-of-way in 1990, rehabilitated a 10-foot wide portion for trail use, and opened it as the Henry Hudson Trail in 1992. In 1993, the Park System secured a Federal ISTEA transportation enhancement grant to repair or replace 11 bridges and install signage along the trail, and it opened the full nine miles in 1995.

By 2000, nearly 60,000 people were hiking, biking, or jogging on the Henry Hudson Trail and enjoying its intermittent views of stream corridors, tidal wetlands, and the Sandy Hook Bay. The Park System secured a Federal grant that year to help extend the Henry Hudson Trail along the Central Railroad of New Jersey's former Matawan to Freehold rail line. Almost 10 miles of this 12-mile southern extension are currently open for use. In 2009, an estimated 180,000 people used the Henry Hudson Trail, and in 2010 readers of *New Jersey Monthly* magazine voted it the Best Biking Trail in New Jersey.

25. Monmouth Cove Marina

1990—10 ACRES; 2009—10.5 ACRES

TO PROTECT the west end of Bayshore Waterfront Park and to help meet the public demand for rental boat slips, the Park System acquired the Gateway Marina in Port Monmouth in 1990 with the help of a Green Acres matching grant. The 1980s housing boom had led to the loss of many rental boat slips as developers converted private marinas into waterside housing clusters. The 10-acre Gateway Marina site (pictured below in 1992, prior to expansion by the Park System) included a boat maintenance shop, fuel and floating docks, storage racks, and considerable frontage along Pews Creek.

The Park System renamed the boating facility as the Monmouth Cove Marina. Today the upgraded Marina operates at full capacity and provides 154 floating wet slips with electric and water, 58 spaces of rack storage plus some land storage, and dockage for transient boaters.

26. Sunnyside Recreation Area

1990–129 ACRES; 2009–135 ACRES

SUNNYSIDE Recreation Area is located in the historic Nut Swamp section of Middletown, which Europeans settled in the late 17th century. A member of one of Middletown's earliest settlement families, Sylvanus Grover, acquired land along the Middletown-Lincroft Road in 1759 and built a small tenant house that today is the oldest section of the extant farmhouse. After George W. Crawford of Holmdel acquired the property in 1856, it became known as Sunnyside Farm. The 135-acre farm remained in the Crawford family until 1933 when Henry and Katherine Neuberger of New York bought it and transformed it into a country estate. The Neubergers renovated the house and some of the barns in the Colonial Revival Style, and they raised pedigreed steers and horses on the farm.

In the 1980s, Middletown Township fought a six-year court battle to prevent Calton Homes from building 1,250 housing units on the farm under the State's Mount Laurel "builder's remedy" program, which allowed builders to increase density in exchange for affordable housing. The Park System

acquired 116 acres in 1990, and Calton Homes donated the remaining 13 acres. Because of its location and suitability for active recreation, the Park System named the new park the Sunnyside Recreation Area.

Situated at the confluence of Nut Swamp Brook and Crooked Run, roughly half of the Park is wetland, a reminder of the old Nut Swamp. The historic Nut Swamp name of the area derives from the wooded wetlands that once extended widely along Nut Swamp Brook and contained an abundance of nut-producing trees. Like the surrounding area, the Sunnyside landscape has been highly transformed by settlement and agriculture. Early farmers drained much of the former wetlands for field crops and livestock pasture, and agriculture continued on the site until the Park System's acquisition.

Nut Swamp Brook runs through the northern portion of the Park and flows to Shadow Lake, which drains to the Navesink River. The brook has remnants of mature American beech/white and red oak forest on its steep slopes and a bottomland of red maple/green ash forest. These bottomlands are late successional woodlands developing on what was pasture or hayfield for several centuries, with mockernut hickory, black walnut, and tulip poplar trees. In the 1990s, Park System ecologists initiated a management plan to restore old field and wetland habitats from the former agricultural land use. Wet meadow and herbaceous fields enhanced with wildflowers and tall prairie grasses now edge Middletown-Lincroft Road that divides the Park, providing a distinct contrast to the equestrian facility and its surrounding paddocks and pastures. A 1.4-mile trail winds through the meadows on the west side of the road.

When the leaders of SPUR (Special People United to Ride) approached Park System officials about expanding their joint therapeutic riding program, which had outgrown the facilities at Huber Woods Park, the officials recommended moving it to Sunnyside. SPUR raised $750,000 in a memorable "Off to the Races" fundraising event in October 2000, and celebrated the opening of the Sunnyside Equestrian Center with the Park System in 2002 with three performances by the Royal Lipizzaner Stallions from Austria. The Equestrian Center includes an 80 ft. by 200 ft. indoor arena, 18 stalls, instructional rooms, and offices.

Each year over 100 SPUR volunteers assist Park System equestrian staff in helping hundreds of people with disabilities enjoy riding. The Equestrian Center also provides riding opportunities and lessons for able-bodied persons. The staff conducts programs for small groups of children and aspiring equestrians in horse care, safety, and riding. They also run an introductory summer camp in the fundamentals of horse-manship, stable chores, and English riding.

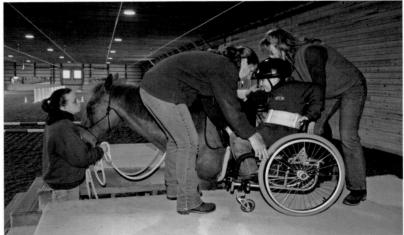

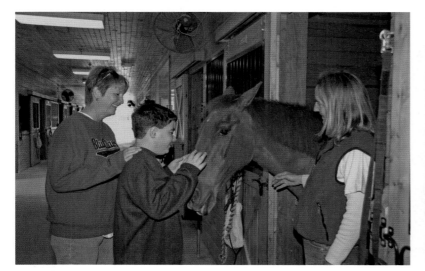

27. Charleston Springs Golf Course

1990–204 ACRES; 2009–781 ACRES

TO PROVIDE a public golfing opportunity in southwestern Monmouth County, the Park System began acquiring suitable land in Millstone Township with its 1990 purchase of the 204-acre Bobbink Nursery founded by the noted horticulturist and rosarian Lambertus Bobbink. In 1992, the Park System purchased 383 acres of the adjacent Bulk Nursery, and the sellers donated an additional 34 acres. Park System staff set the goal of building and operating an environmentally sustainable golf course that would provide a high quality golfing experience, and they hired the nationally-known golf course architects Cornish, Silva and Mungeam of Uxbridge, Massachusetts, to design two 18-hole, par 72 regulation courses for the site to achieve the goal.

Mark Mungeam, the project architect, planned both golf courses to utilize the site's existing terrain, natural features, man-made ponds, and native plants as much as possible. He designed the North Course on the former Bobbink Nursery as a Scottish links-style course with broad undulating fairways defined by water hazards and meadows of native grasses and wildflowers. For the South Course on the former Bulk Nursery, he designed a classic parkland-style course with tree-lined fairways and intermittent native grass meadows. The golf course first opened for play in 1998.

Charleston Springs also has a five-acre Short Game Area for practice and teaching with two chipping greens, a putting green, and bunkers. The full-service Golf Center, designed by architect George Rudolph, complements the landscape. More than just a golf course, Charleston Springs includes 70 acres for other recreational uses, including the 2-mile Stone Bridge Trail that meanders through old fields and a forest along the Manalapan Brook, crossing the historic Sweetman's Stone Bridge. In a 2010 survey, readers of *New Jersey Monthly* magazine selected Charleston Springs Golf Course as one of the Best Public Golf Courses in the State.

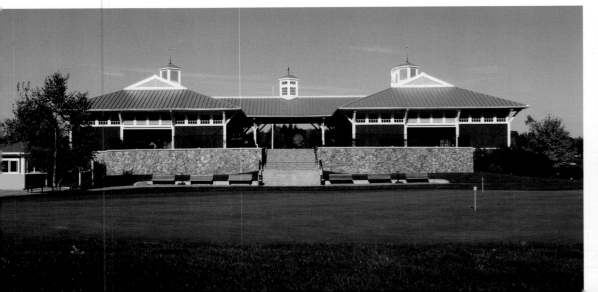

Tributaries of the Manalapan Brook bisect the North and South Courses and flow to the South River, which drains into Raritan Bay. Bulk Lake, adjacent to the South Course on the former Bulk Nursery, originated as a mill pond, and Bobbink Pond on the North Course was created by the former Bobbink Nursery for irrigation. Both nursery sites had been farmed for two centuries or more, and their extensive agricultural fields, limited forest areas, and plentiful water sources provided excellent resources for the new golf course.

To help mitigate the loss of old field habitats in the region, Park System ecologists incorporated nesting bird habitats into the design of the courses. Along the shoreline of new water features they developed aquatic habitats for snipe, long-legged waders, and many aquatic insects. The meadow areas incorporate prairie species such as big and little bluestem, switchgrass, purple coneflower, and coreopsis, all of which provide an attractive backdrop to the fine fescue rough areas. The low maintenance design includes native plantings that require mowing only once a year, need no fertilization, and filter runoff into the ponds, which provide all the water needed for the courses.

Acquisitions of adjacent land have added forest habitat, which includes shrub lands and woodlands developing on former farmland and late successional forest of American beech/red oak uplands and red maple swamp lowlands.

28. Crosswicks Creek Greenway

1990–88 ACRES; 2009–1,480 ACRES

WORKING IN PARTNERSHIP with the County and State farmland preservation program, the Park System envisioned the Greenway as a way to protect the Crosswicks Creek stream corridor and to preserve a significant rural landscape of farms and forest in Upper Freehold Township. Starting with the preservation of Historic Walnford's immediate setting and historic lands to its north, the County gradually expanded the Greenway along the full six miles of the creek that flow through the County and preserved adjacent farms in the stream valley. Together with county parkland, farmland preservation and conservation easements on private property, more than 4,000 acres are permanently protected in the Crosswicks Creek watershed within Monmouth County. Today the Greenway is part of a regional multi-county effort to protect the water quality of this important watershed. From its headwaters in Fort Dix, Crosswicks Creek drains into the Hamilton Marsh at the Delaware River, where freshwater combines with tidal saltwater in a highly diverse habitat supporting over 780 plant species and 230 bird species.

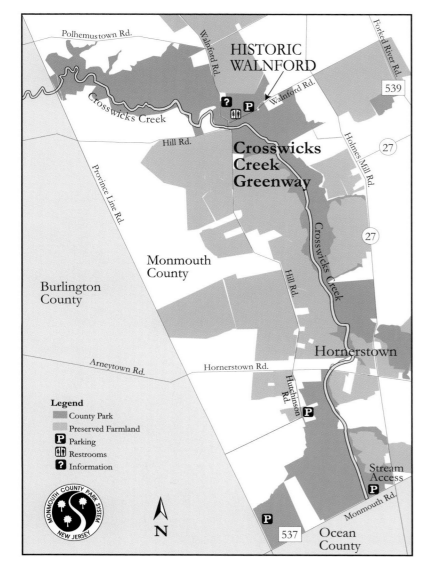

In addition to the riparian areas adjacent to the stream, the parklands within the Crosswicks Creek Greenway include forests and fields that contribute to the area's rural landscape. The historically forested areas of the Greenway maintain exceptional forest quality, with fine examples of rare plants not found elsewhere in the County, including wild rice, wild pinks, green-dragon, lizard's tail, Virginia bluebells, and golden saxifrage perennials, as well as surviving American elm and pumpkin ash trees. The dominant forest communities are red maple swamp with green ash in the bottomlands adjacent to the stream and hickory/white ash in the uplands. A mixed oak/tulip poplar forest community has developed where farming was discontinued. The Park System leases about two-thirds of the fields within the Greenway to farmers and nurseries, and the remaining one-third are natural areas of wet meadows and fields with warm and cool season grasses.

Some of the many wildlife species recorded in the Greenway include American bittern, bald eagle, black-crowned night heron, bobolink, dickcissel, great blue heron, kingfisher, little blue heron, northern harrier, pileated woodpecker, quail, red-tail hawk, wild turkey, wood duck, yellow-crowned night heron, cormorant (pictured right), black and water snakes, and box and painted turtles.

29. Manasquan River Greenway

1990–17 ACRES; 2009–337 ACRES

THE PARK SYSTEM established the Manasquan River Greenway in 1990 to expand the protection of the upper Manasquan watershed, which provides the major source of drinking water in the southern portion of the County. By the end of 2009 the Park System had acquired 51 parcels along the river totaling 337 acres. The Greenway connects Howell Park Golf Course, the Manasquan Reservoir, and Turkey Swamp Park, and the preserved forested wetlands and adjacent uplands protect the riverine habitat for many species, including bald eagles. While some land uses adjacent to the Greenway contribute to excess storm water runoff and pollutants in the river, public officials and watershed managers have developed and implemented strategies to mitigate these impacts.

Characteristic trees in the Greenway include chestnut, scarlet, red, white and black oak, sweet and black gum, pitch pine, and red maple. The dominant shrubs include huckleberry and sweet pepperbush, and significant perennials include trailing arbutus and eastern turkeybeard.

30. Fisherman's Cove Conservation Area

1995–35 ACRES; 2009–55 ACRES

PARK SYSTEM planners identified the privately-owned 35-acre Fisherman's Cove site on the Manasquan River in 1990 as the largest piece of undeveloped land along the County's Atlantic coastline (1992 aerial shown below). A 15-acre filled area of the site had been used for parking for many years, and was zoned for a planned unit development with a maximum of six residential units per acre. The County acquired Fisherman's Cove in 1995 to preserve it from intensive development and to protect the Manasquan River and Deep Creek, a tidal stream that borders the western boundary. Additional acquisitions have preserved adjacent wetlands. The Park System converted an old bait and tackle shop on the property into an Activity Center for environmental programs.

Fisherman's Cove lies within the Outer Coastal Plain, and about 20% of the land consists of tidal communities of mudflat, low salt marsh dominated by smooth cordgrass, and high salt marsh of salt meadow cordgrass, all fringed by the invasive common reed called phragmites. Another 20% of the Park consists of upland dune communities of beachgrass, bayberry, and tidebush, and an interior maritime shrub forest of black cherry, red cedar, and American holly. Fisherman's Cove had been used periodically between 1931 and 1984 as a deposit area for silt dredged from the river, and the balance of the Park is a highly-disturbed urbanized environment largely dominated by phragmites. Park System ecologists implemented a restoration plan in 2005 to control the phragmites and to nurture a maritime forest and shrub habitat.

31. Bel-Aire Golf Course

1997–78 ACRES; 2009–114 ACRES

MORTEN HANSEN, JR., an avid golfer and member of the Manasquan River Golf Club, built Bel-Aire Golf Course on a former crop farm in Wall Township in 1964 in part with money he had won in the Irish Sweepstakes in the 1950s. Hansen designed Bel-Aire himself as a 27-hole executive course with a gently rolling terrain containing an 18-hole, 3,600-yard par 60 course and a 9-hole, 1,350-yard par 3 course. In the 33 years that Hansen and his two sons operated Bel-Aire, it attracted many beginner and older golfers who often prefer to play on executive courses, which have shorter fairways than regulation golf courses.

When the Hansens decided to sell Bel-Aire in 1997, about 60% of the land was zoned for highway business and the remainder was zoned for residential development. Wall Township officials urged the Freeholders to acquire the popular course to preserve it as a major recreation facility at the busy intersection of Routes 34 and 524. Preserving Bel-Aire also protected open space in a highly-developed area and complemented the Park System's earlier acquisition of the Pine Brook Golf Course in Manalapan Township to provide executive-length public golf opportunities in the northwestern portion of the County.

To expand access to golf, Park System golf staff operate more than 200 introductory and intermediate golf clinics annually for adults and juniors at Bel-Aire, Charleston Springs, and Howell Park Golf Courses. The Park System also sponsors Youth Tournaments at these courses where 125 to 150 young players typically participate. With its affordability, accessibility, and ease of play, Bel-Aire attracted the second highest number of golfers among the Park System's six golf courses in 2009.

32. Wolf Hill Recreation Area | 1997–91 ACRES

THE ELEVATED Wolf Hill area of Oceanport may have derived its name from the presence of wolves in the area long ago. Charles W. Billings, the first mayor of Oceanport, acquired the West Farm on Eatontown Boulevard around 1910 and turned it into a country estate with a large Colonial Revival house and a complex of horse and cattle barns. The N.J. Sports and Exposition Authority later acquired the 91-acre Billings Farm in 1963 as a supplement to its adjacent Monmouth Park racetrack, and used the house as a guesthouse for racetrack jockeys and VIPs. Horse trainers exercised their horses on the land, and the Authority built a softball field on it.

The Park System identified the property in 1991 as a potential recreation site to serve a densely populated area of the County and purchased it 1997 from the Sports and Exposition Authority, which had designated it as surplus. Today, the Park has two softball fields, an enclosed off-leash dog area, and large open areas for hiking, and Park System planners have outlined future recreation facilities as well. Along the north boundary an unused railroad right-of-way, targeted as a linear trail greenway in the 2006 "Open Space Plan," offers potential links to Long Branch, Eatontown, and beyond.

Park System ecologists have allowed natural processes to prevail on much of the site's former pasture, paddocks and fields to provide wildlife habitat in a developed area. Killdeer and bobolinks are among the birds that frequent the 52 acres of cool season grassy fields, which are mowed just twice a year, and visitors enjoy walking the paths through the willowy grasses. On the three acres of wet meadow, brant, loons, and greater white-fronted geese have been observed, along with wetland-dependent plants, insects, amphibians, reptiles, and birds. To buffer the surrounding residential areas, the ecologists have reforested portions of the Park's periphery with trees donated by N.J. Tree Foundation.

33. Big Brook Park | 1997–379 ACRES

MARLBORO State Hospital opened in 1931 on land that had been farmed since the 18th century, and the State eventually expanded the site to over 900 acres, partly to provide some farming activities for patients. When the State announced plans to close the psychiatric hospital in the 1980s, the Park System began negotiations to acquire the farmland south of Route 520 for conservation and recreation and acquired 379 acres in 1997. The undeveloped Park borders Big Brook, which drains to the Swimming River Reservoir, and contains almost 200 acres of gently rolling fields divided by hedgerows and wooded drainages. The cool season fields of smooth brome grass and the warm season fields of native broom sedge, golden-rod, and other perennials provide a rare contiguous field habitat for several priority species of field nesting birds, including grasshopper sparrow, harrier, and bobolink. The forested areas include a young wetland forest developing along the drainages and 50 acres of maturing American beech-white oak-tulip poplar-hickory forest on the hillsides.

Right top and middle: Big Brook Park; *right bottom:* DeBois Creek Recreation Area.

34. DeBois Creek Recreation Area

1998–109 ACRES; 2009–165 ACRES

WHEN a 109-acre sod farm zoned for industrial use on Route 33 in Freehold Town-ship became available in 1998, the Park System acquired it to protect water supply and to preserve it for future recreation opportunities for the populated Freehold area. DeBois Creek runs along the east boundary and Bunker Creek runs along the west, and both drain to the Manasquan River above the Manasquan Reservoir. About 21 acres of woods line DeBois Creek, but the majority of the undeveloped park site is open and flat. A 12-acre field of warm season grasses provides wildlife habitat on the western portion of the property, and the Park System leases the remaining field areas for sod farming and field crops. As adjacent land is devel-oped, the stream protection in this Park will become increasingly important. The northeast corner of the Park borders the unused Freehold to Farmingdale railroad right-of-way, which could be reactivated someday but in the meantime provides a potential trail access to these communities.

35. Union Transportation Trail

1998–1.5 ACRES; 2009–6 ACRES

INVESTORS established the Pemberton and Hightstown Railroad in 1864 as a short line to provide dairies and farms along its route with access to larger railroads at junctions in Pemberton in Burlington County and Hightstown in Mercer County (route shown on 1873 map below). The Union Transportation Company acquired the line in 1888, and it prospered for many years until the construction of the New Jersey Turnpike in the 1950s cut it off from Hightstown. Portions of the line continued operating until 1976, and Jersey Central Power & Light later acquired the right-of-way. Park System planners identified the 8.6-mile right-of-way through Upper Freehold Township as a possible rail trail in their 1991 "Park, Recreation and Open Space Plan." The Park System leased the right-of-way in 1998 from JCP&L for 99 years, which also preserves it for potential reactivation as a rail corridor. The opening of the first two miles of the trail in 2010 includes the rehabilitation of an historic wood trestle bridge over Lahaway Creek in Hornerstown, one of the few physical remnants of the old railroad (pictured right in 20th century).

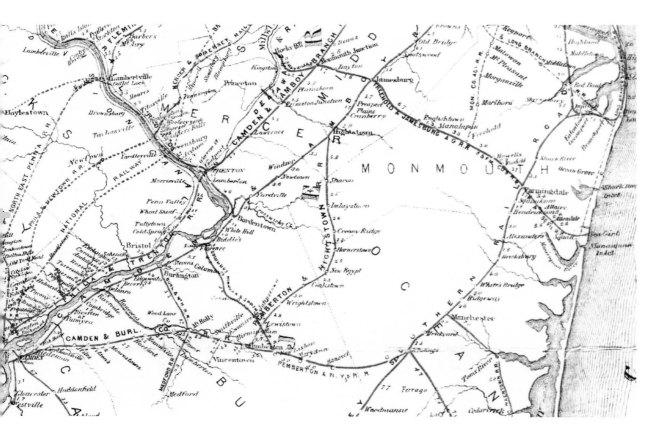

36. Perrineville Lake Park

1999–93 ACRES; 2009–929 ACRES

PARK SYSTEM planners recommended County acquisition of a large amount of open land around Perrineville Lake in Millstone Township in the 1991 "Monmouth County Park, Recreation and Open Space Plan" for a new regional park to preserve Perrineville Lake and its rural environs, and to provide recreational opportunities in a developing area of the County. The 15-acre lake originated as a mill pond on a tributary of Rocky Brook, which drains to the Millstone River, a major source of drinking water in central New Jersey. The Park System secured a Green Acres matching grant to acquire the first 93 acres in 1999 and with the help of additional Green Acres grants and supporters of open space preservation in Millstone Township, has expanded the Park by a factor of 10 in just 10 years. By the end of 2009, this was the fifth largest park in the Park System.

In the 20th century, local proprietors operated a summertime resort on Perrineville Lake, which is the Park's scenic landmark and a favorite spot of local fishermen. Nearly five miles of park trails extend through forests, along fields, and around the lake, and these are particularly popular with local equestrians. The Park incorporates a significant portion of the historic greenbelt of the New Deal planned community of Roosevelt, and extends to the State's 6,323-acre Assunpink Wildlife Management Area.

The Park System leases 75% of the Park's 310 acres of fields for agricultural use with stipulations for mowed perimeters for public and maintenance access. Ecologists manage the remaining field acreage as natural areas of native grasses and other herbaceous plants to preserve wildlife habitat within a larger area of agricultural and fallow lands. Altogether these lands provide a regional habitat for some species of concern, including eastern box turtle, grasshopper sparrow, and bobolink. Spotted turtles inhabit wetland areas in the Park, and wild turkeys are commonly sighted. The Park's grassland habitat also hosts American kestrel, eastern bluebird, meadowlark, northern bobwhite, and quail.

Woodlands constitute about two-thirds of the Park, including both young and mature forest. The oldest forested portions of the Park contain red maple and black gum in wetland areas south of the lake, and old growth chestnut oak and mixed oak elsewhere. Species sighted in these forests include wood thrush, veery, red-headed woodpecker, northern parula, brown thrasher, black-throated green warbler, and eastern box turtle. Woodlands emerging on former agricultural land host black locust, sassafras, American beech, sweet gum, sweet birch, white ash, black cherry, mockernut hickory, and tulip poplar trees. Sweet pepperbush, blueberry, and black raspberry shrubs are also prominent in the Park.

37. Metedeconk River Greenway

1999–93 ACRES; 2009–121 ACRES

IN THE 1991 "Monmouth County Park, Recreation and Open Space Plan," the Park System designated the Metedeconk River as a critical stream corridor for the protection of water quality and wildlife. While most of the river forms the border between Monmouth and Ocean Counties, the Plan identified the Metedeconk's North Brook tributary, which flows from Turkey Swamp Park to the border, as a greenway for County acquisition to protect and buffer floodplains from adjacent land use and development. The Park System is preserving land along the Metedeconk stream corridor in conjunction with similar efforts in the Ocean County portion of the watershed.

38. Yellow Brook Tract | 2000–225 ACRES; 2009–338 ACRES

THE PARK SYSTEM began preserving this important forest land in Howell Township near the U.S. Naval Weapons Station Earle in 2000 with the purchase of 142 acres and the sellers' donation of 83 adjacent acres. The Park protects part of the Yellow Brook, a major tributary of the Manasquan River above the Manasquan Reservoir. The tract lies at the junction of the Pine Barrens to the south, where the sandy soil holds water and provides filtration, and the upland hardwood forest to the north, which generally drains more quickly. Most of the tract is forested wetland with pitch pine/red maple and Atlantic white cedar swamp communities. The limited upland areas have predominantly pitch pine and black, white and scarlet oak. The cedar swamp contains Collin's sedge, which is threatened or endangered through most of its coastal range. The Park also contains a remnant cranberry bog, which has developed into a scrub-shrub wetland community.

Bibliography

Monmouth County Park System Publications and Reports:

"2002 Park District Forum Resource Book," Monmouth County Park System, June 2002.

"Amendment to the Monmouth County Park, Recreation and Open Space Plan," Monmouth County Park System, March 1998.

Annual Reports, Monmouth County Park System, 1968 to 2009.

"Annual Report of the Organization and Activities of the Monmouth County Park System," Monmouth County Park System, March 1992.

"Answer Book—A Guide to Our Parks and Park Offerings," Monmouth County Park System, November 1995.

Attendance Figures for Monmouth County Parks, 1961 to 2009.

Calendar of Events and Activity Directory, Monmouth County Park System, 1970s to present.

Fowler, Michael, and Seigelman, Howard, "Monmouth County Park System Management Summary: Citizen's Survey," Monmouth County Park System, November 16, 1984.

Friends of the Parks Newsletter, Vol. 1, No. 1, March 1992 to present.

Green Heritage, Monmouth County Park System, Vol. 9, No. 8, August 1975 to Vol. 44, No. 1, Spring, 2010.

Green Link, Vol. 1, No. 1, September–October 1977 to March–April, 2010.

"Guide to Parks and Services," Monmouth County Park System, c1986.

"Inclusion Philosophy and Process," Monmouth County Park System, October 2002.

"Mission Statements," Various Departments and Divisions, Monmouth County Park System, December 2002.

"Monmouth County Coastal Waterfront Access Study," Monmouth County Park System, December 1992.

Monmouth County Historic Preservation Guide, Monmouth County Park System, 1989.

Monmouth County Historic Sites Inventory, Summary Report, Monmouth County Park System, 1990.

"Monmouth County Open Space Guide," Monmouth County Park System, January 1983.

"Monmouth County Open Space Plan," Monmouth County Park System and the Monmouth County Planning Board, January 1971.

Monmouth County Open Space Plan, Monmouth County Park System, August 2006.

"Monmouth County Open Space Program," Monmouth County Park System, June 2004.

Monmouth County Park, Recreation and Open Space Plan, Monmouth County Park System, June 1991.

"Monmouth County Recreation Services Guide," Monmouth County Park System, 1989.

Monmouth County Resident Survey Analysis, Monmouth County Park System, December 1996.

"Oceanfront Study," Monmouth County Park System, October 1980.

"Outdoor Group Adventurers, Program Developers Guidebook," Monmouth County Park System, c1980.

"Park Development and Maintenance Plan," Monmouth County Park System, February 2003.

"Recreation Services Plan," Monmouth County Park System, 2001.

"Study of Regional Recreation Needs in the Major Population Centers of Monmouth County, Summary," August 1991.

"Urban Recreation," Monmouth County Park System, 2007.

Monmouth County Planning Board Publications and Reports:

"Bayshore Access Plan," Prepared by the Trust For Public Land for the Monmouth County Planning Board, February 1987 Draft.

Growth Management Guide: Monmouth County, New Jersey, Monmouth County Planning Board, October 1982.

"Monmouth County Profile 2000," Monmouth County Planning Board, 2000.

"Recreation Study and Plan: Monmouth Coastal Region," Monmouth County Planning Board, December 1960.

"Year 2000 Population Projections: A Technical Report to the Board," Monmouth County Planning Board, January 1971.

Publications and Reports by Others:

Catania, Michael F., and Edmund W. Stiles, "Analysis of County Park Systems in New Jersey, Prepared for the Morris County Parks and Conservation Foundation," The Eagleton Institute of Politics, Rutgers University, December 1991.

"Citizen Opinion and Interest Survey, Findings Report," Conducted for the Monmouth County Park System by Leisure Vision/ETC Institute, March 2009.

"The Common Wealth of New Jersey: Outdoor Recreation Resources Plan, Summary," New Jersey Department of Environmental Protection, 1989.

"The Cost of Community Services in Monmouth County, New Jersey," Commissioned by the Monmouth Conservation Foundation, American Farmland Trust, 1998.

"Monmouth County Park System 10th Year Re-Accreditation, 2003," Commission for Accreditation of Park and Recreation Agencies, National Recreation and Park Association.

"Monmouth County Park System Leisure Service Market Study," Brookdale Community College, January 15, 1981.

"Outdoor Recreation Plan of New Jersey, Summary," New Jersey Department of Environmental Protection, 1984.

"Report of Adult Component of Public Interest Survey for the Monmouth County Park System," Management Learning laboratories, June 2003.

"Where the Pavement Ends," Regional Plan Association, December 1987.

Miscellaneous

Accomando, Peter R., and Michelle M. Liebau, "Essex County Park System Celebrates 100 Years of Beauty and Service," *Parks and Recreation*, March 1995.

A Triangle of Land: A History of the Site and Founding of Brookdale Community College, Lincroft, N.J.: Brookdale Community College, 1978.

Breden, T.F., Y.R. Alger, K.S. Walz, A.G. Windisch, *Classification of Vegetation Communities of New Jersey: Second Iteration*, Association for Biodiversity Information and New Jersey Natural Heritage Program, Office of Natural Lands Management, Division of Parks and Forestry, NJ Dept. of Environmental Protection. Trenton, NJ., 2001.

Collins, R.B., and K. H. Anderson, *Plant Communities of New Jersey*, Rutgers University Press, 1994.

Harken, Donald, Sherri Evans, Marc Evans and Kay Harker, *Landscape Restoration Handbook*, United States Golf Association and New York Audubon Society, 1993.

Meeting Minutes of the Monmouth County Board of Chosen Freeholders, Monmouth County Planning Board, and the Monmouth County Board of Recreation Commissioners. Monmouth County Archives.

Monmouth County Park System Land Acquisition Records, Acquisition and Design Department.

Newspaper Clipping Files on the Monmouth County Park System from the *Newark Star Ledger, Asbury Park Press, Red Bank Register*, and *The New York Times*. Monmouth County Archives and Monmouth County Park System.

Truncer, James J., "A Critical Analysis of New Jersey's Green Acres Bond Program," Michigan State University, Department of Resource Development, Special Problems 880, December 1964.

Truncer, James J., "What Should be the Greater Priority in Monmouth and Ocean Counties, Continued Development or the Preservation of Open Space?" May 6, 1985.

Weir, L.H., Editor, *Parks: A Manual of Municipal and County Parks*, New York, A.S. Barnes & Company, 1928.